CLASSIC
TEQUILA

CLASSIC TEQUILA

IAN WISNIEWSKI

First published in 1998 in Great Britain by
Prion Books Limited
32-34 Gordon House Road,
London NW5 1LP

© PRION BOOKS LIMITED
Text copyright © Ian Wisniewski 1998
Designed by DW Design

A CIP record for this book is available from the
British Library

ISBN 1-85375-296-7

Cover design: Bob Eames
Printed in China

CONTENTS

INTRODUCTION

Why is it that we all like to blame our worst alcoholic excess on tequila – as though it's the fault of the drink rather than the drinker? Additional propaganda is equally damning: "it's the one with the worm" and "it's made from a cactus" are two choice examples. Mezcal, a related but separate Mexican speciality, has the worm; and tequila is actually distilled from agave.

Agave also yields the even more historic *pulque* from which tequila is descended, pulque having been a favourite of the Aztecs and other native Indian tribes. When the Spanish *conquistadors* began colonising Mexico in the early 16th century, they introduced the art of distillation, which turned pulque into a prototype tequila.

It's a wonder that a plant as hostile as agave ever became such an integral part of Mexican life. Being classified as a "succulent" disguises its true nature: its incredibly tough, rapier-shaped leaves are also trimmed with vicious needles. They can lacerate anything that gets too close, as I know to my cost.

Tequila is produced from the blue agave, only one of Mexico's couple of hundred varieties of

Opposite
In the popular Hollywood imagination, "south of the border" has always been a mythical party paradise fueled by mariachis and margaritas.

agave. It is a native of the state of Jalisco, which is also home to the *charro*, the aristocratic Mexican cowboy, and the fabulous *mariachi*, the traditional musicians in wide-brimmed hats.

Long established as the national drink of Mexico, tequila is now becoming an international phenomenon, as distillers redefine its niche in the market by combining a centuries-old heritage with a more experimental, creative approach. Indeed, every element of the production process is constantly under review in the drive for greater brand individuality, including the method of cultivating and preparing agave for fermentation, the variety of yeast used, the strength at which the spirit is distilled, the type of barrels, and the degree of ageing. The results are some sensational tequilas that capitalise on the characteristics of agave – earthy, vegetal, herbaceous, spicy and even fruity notes – which can be further enhanced through barrel ageing.

Meanwhile, the growing popularity of Mexican and Tex-Mex food is helping to show how well tequila can partner its national, as well as international, cuisine. The current fashion for cocktails is another asset, with tequila thriving on its mixability, and the Margarita now established as an icon of the cocktail set.

So, how far can tequila go ? Actually, all the way.

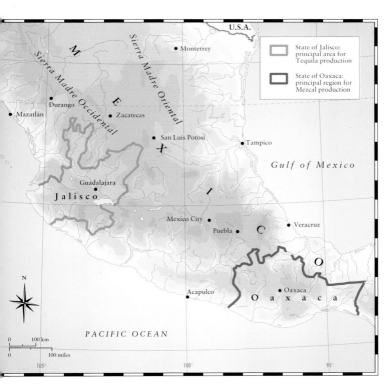

State of Jalisco:
principal area for
Tequila production

State of Oaxaca:
principal region for
Mezcal production

Once dismissed as an "ignoble" spirit compared to
the aristocratic clique that includes Cognac and
malt whisky, tequila is now able to enthral
connoisseurs as readily as it entices newcomers.
Tequila also benefits from a flamboyant, fun-loving
image no other spirit can command. Indeed, it is
poised to fulfil an ancient Aztec philosophy:
"Whenever you specialise and remain focused on
your origins, a cult status is bound to follow."

THE HISTORY AND CULTURE OF TEQUILA

The earliest alcoholic drinks were produced by fermenting various types of vegetation, including plants, grains and fruits, a practice on which the American Indians of Mesoamerica capitalised by using local raw materials. Fermenting a corn-based liquid to produce *tesguino* was one option, while *tuba* was prepared by fermenting palm juice and palm flowers with coconut juice. However, their most important alcoholic drink was pulque, from the fermented sap of an agave plant.

A prehistoric plant, agave has been utilised in various ways by American Indian tribes for at least 10,000 years: the thorns that line the edges of the plant's leaves were their needles and pins; and woven agave fibres produced baskets, mats and cloth. And even though the Indians were cultivating corn from around 5,000 BC, followed by avocados, beans, peppers, squashes and tomatoes, as well as raising turkeys, chewed

remains of the agave indicate that it was also used as an emergency food source if the harvest failed – its bulbous "heart" could be roasted and eaten. In fact, it is thought that the earliest nomadic Indians depended on the wild agave to such an extent that they frequently settled wherever it was most plentiful. Moreover, even ancient cultures such as the Tula and Teotihuacan travelled with agave seeds, and settled in the type of terrain considered the most advantageous for its cultivation.

Agave leaves were used to produce a type of parchment, on which important events and tribal

Above
An allegorical fresco by Diego Rivera depicts the genesis of the Aztec empire. Agave has been central to Mexican culture and rituals for over 10,000 years.

histories and cultures were recorded. These records include references to the agave's various uses, which feature in codices (illustrated manuscripts) such as the Tonalmatlnahuatl, Florentine and Borgia. The Codex Boutturini, for instance, describes the history of the Aztecs as they migrated across Mexico – and how they learned to produce pulque – before founding Tenochtitlan, on the site of what became Mexico City. Unbridled consumption of what is thought to be pulque is also the subject of murals dating from 200 BC at the site of the Great Pyramid of Cholula that were uncovered in the late 1960s.

Exactly where, when and how pulque was first produced is impossible to determine, though various legends (often an entertaining source) offer explanations. Common to them all is the "divine" origin of pulque, particularly as early civilisations believed agave to be the first plant created by the gods.

According to Aztec legend, the gods sent a bolt of lightning, which struck an agave plant. Not only did this split the agave into two perfect halves, but the heat generated by the lightning also cooked the heart of the plant. The Aztecs assumed the aromatic sap oozing from the plant was the lightning transformed into a "nectar". The belief that it was a gift from the gods was reinforced by an unexpectedly sweet flavour.

Then again, the origins of pulque may stem from a poor harvest (perhaps a less direct act of the gods) that drove the Indians to turn to agave, which had to be cooked before it could be consumed. Apparently, while the plants were cooking in deep bonfire pits, a rainstorm filled the pits with water. Several days of sunshine followed and the liquid in the pits began to ferment. When this liquid was tasted, a state of intoxication soon followed, which was deemed to be a transcendental condition bestowed by the gods.

Consequently, pulque's role was spiritual and initially its consumption was confined to religious ceremonies. Social drinking was prohibited, and drunkenness was punishable by death. Indeed, the mystical state of intoxication through pulque enabled priests to commune directly with the gods, as well as to banish evil spirits.

A particular object of this devotion was the goddess Mayahuel, who symbolised the fertility of the earth. Having been turned into an agave, she was also goddess of this plant and its sap was considered the equivalent of her breast milk. Apparently she nurtured her 400 offspring from her 400 breasts, which begs the question of where they all were. Illustrations often depict Mayahuel wearing a nose ring, and having long red hair, but no breasts are ever in sight. But, then, who are we to wonder? She was after all a goddess.

However, Mayahuel hardly enjoyed a monopoly. Among several other gods of pulque, Tepoztecatl was also the god of alcoholic excess, while Xochiquetzal represented a more interesting

combination, being the goddess of both drunkenness and sexuality (which can't have been the first time the two have been linked).

Priests weren't the only ones to be permitted pulque. Religious ceremonies regularly involved human sacrifice and pulque was served to the victims too. They must certainly have needed something alcoholic before Aztec priests ripped out their hearts, using knives made from shafts of volcanic glass. A good dose of pulque would have gone a long way towards minimising resistance. This type of sacrifice sounds barbaric, but the rationale was that a blood sacrifice ensured the continuation of "gifts" from such deities as the sun god Huitzilopochti, to ensure the sun would rise on the following day.

The agave's versatility also served the priesthood in other ways: important religious events were recorded on agave parchment; and Toltec priests, for whom self-mutilation was an integral element of their faith, used agave needles to draw their own blood.

Religious ceremonies equally utilised other plants. Reflecting the principles of pulque, the mezcal cactus was eaten for its hallucinogenic qualities, the resulting visions also being considered transcendental. Moreover, vast cacti barrels (the main trunk of a plant) served another purpose: the Aztecs used them as altars upon which to lay sacrificial victims.

Beyond religious ceremonies, pulque later became a drink of the military and the ruling élite, helping to provide courage in battles and being served as a toast with which to celebrate victory. A Toltec nobleman called Papantzin, whose social rank entitled him to prepare pulque for his own consumption, is the source of another legendary tale. Being an ambitious father, he wanted to see his daughter Princess Xochitl advantageously married. Consequently, armed with a batch of pulque, she was dispatched to try and charm King Tepacaltzin (AD 990—1042). Maybe the pulque helped, or maybe it was surplus to the princess's other assets – history doesn't record the details – but the king fell deeply in love with the princess, they soon married and, needless to say, lived happily ever after.

Opposite

Pulque, tequila's ancient ancestor, was thought to be a gift from the Gods – and the state it offered transcendental. It came to play a key role in human sacrificial rituals and many other important religious ceremonies.

The standard method for producing pulque is though to have been devised by the Otomíes, whose god of pulque was also their water god. They were among central Mexico's earliest settlers and renowned for consuming of vast quantities of pulque. Their production method consisted of burning wood in deep, stone-lined pits until only embers remained. Agave hearts, trimmed of leaves, were then arranged on top of the hot stones so as to leave a central opening, with a top layer of agave hearts covered with agave leaves and soil. Water was poured into the opening, which was subsequently sealed with a log. The water turned to steam on contact with the hot stones, so regular additions of water meant the agaves steam-cooked in the course of a day. The agaves cooled for a further day and were then removed from the pit and beaten vigourously with wooden clubs to extract the sap, which was left to ferment naturally in the open air.

A simpler method of producing pulque avoided the bother of harvesting and cooking the agaves by collecting sap directly from the plants. The Tula and Teotihuacan Indians, for example, used knives fashioned from volcanic glass to lacerate the surface of the agave heart. This released the sap, which was either consumed fresh or allowed to ferment into pulque. Another method entailed slicing off the stalk that emerges when the agave is about to flower. By inserting a hollow reed in the indentation left by the stalk, the sap could be sucked out from the heart. The Ticuila Indians also prepared a type of pulque by fermenting water in which roasted agave leaves had been infused.

SPANISH COLONIALISM DAWNS

The Aztecs had migrated across central Mexico looking for a prophetic vision – an eagle, perched on a cactus, eating a snake. This was a sign from the gods to indicate where they should settle in order to enjoy prosperity and freedom. The settlement founded during the 13th century developed into Tenochtitlan, capital of an Aztec empire that subsequently comprised most of central Mexico. Indeed, Tenochtitlan was a sophisticated city, with a system of streets laid out in the form of a grid and a population of more than 200,000.

Hernando Cortés, already a veteran of Spanish colonialism having participated in the conquest of Cuba in 1511, reached Tenochtitlan in 1519. He landed on the Yucatan coast, accompanied by several hundred Spanish conquistadors. Cortés was received by the reigning emperor, Montezuma, who initially believed Cortés to be Quetzalcoatl ("the feathered serpent"), the god of

Above
Although Cortés and the Spanish ransacked Aztec culture, they did bring with them distillation techniques that would eventually turn the simple brew of pulque into tequila.

learning and the priesthood. According to Aztec legend, Quetzalcoatl had set sail for Tula Tlapallan ("the land of red and black"), promising to return in a year that marked the beginning of a *ce acatl* time cycle, which signified important life-changes. The year 1519 just happened to be the beginning of such a cycle.

Montezuma was then about 40 years old, and was described as strikingly handsome – tall, well built, stylishly attired, his long hair immaculately groomed and his beard trimmed. With so many attributes, it's not surprising that, in addition to his two wives, Montezuma had a legion of concubines who apparently bore him 150 children. According to *The True History of the Conquest of*

New Spain written by Bernal Diaz del Castillo, one of the conquistadors accompanying Cortés, Montezuma was typically served gourmet dishes throughout the day, most of which, presumably, were not consumed. This included various game birds like quail and partridge, seafood such as lobster and shrimp, grasshoppers, and ants' eggs. Montezuma offered Cortés a drink made from cocoa beans, ground corn and tlixochitl (better known as vanilla pods), sweetened with honey. He also gave him an illuminated manuscript depicting Aztec history and culture.

Montezuma continued to rule for a while, but his imprisonment by Cortés eventually led to an Aztec rebellion, forcing Cortés to retreat to a Spanish stronghold in Veracruz. Cortés gathered reinforcements and returned. Although the Aztecs greatly outnumbered the Spanish, the latter had the advantage of firearms and horses, and many Indians who had been oppressed by the Aztecs swelled the Spanish ranks. Cortés defeated the Aztecs and captured Tenochtitlan in 1521. The city was destroyed and the Aztec ruins were used as the foundation stones for the capital of New Spain, which would later become Mexico City.

The conquistadors had brought with them supplies of wine and brandy from Spain, and perhaps also a prototype rum from the Caribbean islands, such as Hispaniola, which were being colonised. Moreover, as governor of New Spain from 1521 to 1527, Cortés tried to ensure future wine supplies by planting vines of the mission grape imported from Spain, though even before these vines yielded grapes, wine of a sort was being produced from wild vines. However, the conquistadors were forced to supplement their supply of imported wines and spirits by turning to local specialities. Pulque was sampled and dismissed as an unpalatable native drink. Moreover, at around 5 per cent abv, pulque was far weaker than the drinks the Spanish were used to.

The only solution was to fortify pulque by distilling it. While this process was unknown to the Aztecs, the Spanish are thought to have learned the principles of distillation from the Moors in as early as the 8th century. The Spanish initially referred to this spirit as either *aguardiente* (a generic term for spirits), *vino de mezcal*, or *vino de maguey* (maguey being the Spanish term for agave, which replaced the original Indian name of *metl*).

Whichever name was used, the manner of serving it was almost immediately standardised, with hollowed-out cattle horns used as drinking vessels. This tradition has continued in some distilleries, where a cattle horn is still used to sample tequila straight from the still.

As pulque was produced from various species of agave, the conquistadors began to experiment with different types of pulque. And as the conquest of Mexico continued, the Spaniards reached the region of Chimalhuacan in western

Mexico, where the states of Jalisco, Colima, Nayarit and Aguascalientes are now found. There the Ticuila Indians were producing pulque from blue agave, which the conquistadors found yielded the finest spirit. As blue agave is native to the state of Jalisco, production began to be centred around the town of Tequila. The Ticuila Indians, a Nahuatl-speaking tribe, had founded the town of Tequila in 1530 on the site of an earlier Indian settlement. As the town is near a dormant volcano, it is thought the word tequila is Nahuatl for "volcano" or, more specifically, "lava hill". It is also possible that tequila meant "place of work" (which would be equally suitable for the centre of tequila production), or "place of wild herbs".

However, after its initial flourish, distilling pulque was outlawed by various periods of prohibition in an attempt to protect the consumption of Spanish wines and spirits in Mexico. Needless to say, this legislation only resulted in illicit distilling. And, while the Spanish may have observed the law and continued to drink wines and spirits from their homeland, the locals, who had gained a taste for agave spirit, did not. Consequently, it was decided that the revenue gained from taxing locally produced alcohol would offset any decline in the consumption of Spanish wines and spirits. Indeed, by the 1540s taxes were already being collected by the Intendencia, which was responsible for collecting taxes for the King of Spain.

From this time the indigenous Nahuatl Indians were being converted to Catholicism, with priests in the town of Tequila also appropriating from the Indians the land upon which they established haciendas – meaning a family chapel within the main building – and distillation was principally confined to haciendas at that period. Nevertheless, Spain still sought to protect domestic wine production, and in 1595 Philip II prohibited the planting of any new vines in Mexico, or even the replanting of existing vines.

Domingo Lazara de Arregui, a clergyman visiting the province of Nueva Galicia in 1620 (of which Guadalajara was the capital, and Tequila an important outpost), wrote of the agave: "Once cooked they can also be pressed to squeeze out the must, and this is distilled to produce a liquor clearer than water and more powerful than aguardiente. Although … it confers many virtues, the excessive manner in which it is consumed debases the wine and the plant."

It wasn't until 1753 that the first commercial distillery, La Antigua Cruz ('The Old Cross') was established, by Pedro Sanchez de Tagle on his estate, the Hacienda de Cuisillos. The agave

spirit produced was then known as *chinguerite*, or "mezcal wine". Another commercial distillery, the Hacienda Corralejo, was established in 1755 in Penjamo, in the state of Guanjuato. However, a further period of prohibition followed from 1785 to 1795, instigated by King Carlos III, in order to protect Spanish alcoholic drinks.

The repeal of prohibition in 1795 was marked by another Spaniard, Don José Maria Guadalupe Cuervo, who established a distillery that also used cultivated rather than wild agave. The

Above
The fountain at La Antigua Cruz, the first commercial tequila distillery – established in 1753.

23

distillery of José Cuervo (which sounds better when not translated into Joe Crow) continued to thrive, remaining family-owned and the world's top selling tequila brand.

During the late 18th and early 19th centuries, consumers in Mexico City and other parts of Mexico began to acknowledge that the finest aguardiente de agave, as it was then popularly known, was produced around the town of Tequila. This resulted in the name of the town being increasingly used as a reference for the spirit. But political instability and continual insurrections during the 19th century stunted the development of the tequila industry. In 1822, after more than 10 years of civil war, Mexico gained independence from Spanish rule, and it was proclaimed a republic in 1824.

J.C. Beltrami, an Italian explorer touring Jalisco, wrote in 1823: "Tequila is a beautiful town, but it is surrounded by what seems a barren region to the eyes of a European. However, in Mexico, even poor land produces fruit and riches; the maguey (agave) and other indigenous plants have provided Tequila with a prosperity that grains could not. The maguey produces a superb liquor called mezcal wine." Similarly, W.H. Hardy, an English entrepreneur who visited Jalisco in 1825, wrote: "Three leagues to the northwest of Guadalajara is the flourishing town of Tequila, surrounded by gardens and sugar plantations and a variety of maguey (agave). This maguey plant is fermented and distilled into a whisky."

In 1835 Texas declared its independence from Mexico, and became part of the United States in 1845. During the subsequent war with the USA in 1847—48, American troops occupied Mexico City, with a treaty resulting in Mexico ceding certain northern territories. Another bout of civil war followed, which resulted in a European expeditionary force of Spanish, French and British troops being sent in 1862 to Mexico to protect European interests. The British and Spanish troops withdrew from Mexico, but the French advanced and reached Mexico City in 1863, which they occupied until 1867.

I.F. Elton, an Englishman who toured Mexico in the 1860s with the French army, recorded in his diary: "The eternal maguey ... from which is extracted a white, milky juice, and when fermented this becomes the wine of the country. One cannot but walk a few yards without coming across this plant."

Greater stability ensued when General Porfirio Diaz ruled Mexico during 1876—1910, with around a dozen tequila distilleries operating in the 1870s. A significant newcomer was Tequila Sauza, established in 1873 when Don Cenobio Sauza purchased La Antigua Cruz hacienda, the site of the first commercial tequila distillery, and built a new distillery named La Perseverancia. It was also in the mid and late 19th century that

Above

Don Cenobio Sauza – pioneer of important innovations in the early production of tequila.

agave cultivation began in the highlands of Jalisco, with the first distillery established in this region in 1880 by the Torres Perez Vargas family on their hacienda, called Centinela.

Meanwhile, the export industry began to develop in the late 19th century, facilitated by the railway link between Guadalajara and Mexico City. The first recorded exports were to the USA in 1873, when three barrels of José Cuervo were sent to El Paso in Texas. Tequila

Sauza also sent three barrels and two earthenware jars of tequila to New Mexico in the same year. International recognition followed, although tequila was still known under various names. José Cuervo was awarded a medal by the French Republic at the 1889 Paris Exposition, while a so-called "agave brandy" from the town of Tequila won an award at the 1893 Chicago World Fair.

The traditional method of producing tequila continued for most of the 19th century. This meant that the agave hearts were carried by mules to stone-lined pits that served as ovens in the fields. Burning wood in the pits heated the stones, and when only embers remained, piñas (agave hearts) were arranged on top of the stones, covered with agave leaves and soil leaving a central opening. At regular intervals, water was poured through this opening on to the stones, the opening being resealed with a log. The resulting steam cooked the agave, a process that lasted about a day. A further day was allowed for the piñas to cool. The cooked agave hearts were then transported by mule to the distillery, where they were crushed using a *tahona* – a vast stone wheel, attached to a central pole, pulled by mules, horses or cattle around a stone-lined pit to crush the piñas. Both the agave juice and the crushed pulp were transferred to wooden fermentation vats. A distillery worker stood inside the vats and trod the agave fibres to release more juice and to distribute the fermenting

Opposite
*Both the
border
bootlegging years
of Prohibition
and the romance
of the burgeoning
Mexican cinema
in the 1930s
helped to boost
demand for
tequila in
the USA – still
by far its biggest
export market.*

agent – usually three or four day-old pieces of cooked agave. The fermented agave juice and agave pulp were subsequently transferred by means of wooden buckets carried on the head to a copper pot still.

Nevertheless, technical advances during the late 19th century saw distillers beginning to cook agaves at the distillery (then known as *tabernas*) in specially constructed ovens, rather than in the fields. Quality was also greatly improved by distilling twice rather than once, while Don Cenobio Sauza introduced the indirect heating of pot stills using steam coils, rather than direct fire, which subsequently became standard practice.

The Spanish flu epidemic, which struck Mexico after the First World War, also resulted in a boost for tequila as numerous doctors prescribed it, to be taken with salt and lime juice, as a cure. Whether this actually effected any cures is unknown, but it must have made the symptoms more bearable.

During Prohibition in the USA, which prevented the production and importation of alcoholic beverages during 1919—1933, unofficial exports of tequila flourished, with massive quantities being smuggled across the Mexican border. The 1930s and 1940s also saw a boom in Mexican cinema, which gave tequila a flamboyant and romantic image that helped to boost sales in the USA and Europe. Tequila also enjoyed increased demand from the USA during the

Second World War, when exports of Scotch whisky from the United Kingdom were reduced.

It was also during the Second World War that tequila producers first attempted to protect the name of tequila, and to give the spirit a legal definition, so that the name would apply only to tequila produced within the state of Jalisco. However, the first regulations governing production weren't introduced until 1974, when the government established a denomination of origin for tequila – demarcating a 200 sq km production zone in Jalisco.

The most important regulations, the Norma Oficial del Tequila (known as the NORMAS), were passed in 1976 and detailed every aspect of tequila production. The delimited area in which blue agave could be cultivated and in which tequila could be distilled was extended beyond the zone established in 1974 to cover the entire state of Jalisco (comprising just over 78,000 sq km). The NORMAS additionally allowed for blue agave to be cultivated and tequila produced within certain municipalities of the states of Guanajuato, Michoacan, Nayarit and Tamaulipas. The reason for extending the delimited area beyond Jalisco was a boom in the industry dating from the mid 1960s, and the consequent need for greater quantities of agave. Nayarit, Michoacan and Guanajuato border Jalisco: the inclusion of Tamaulipas was more of a surprise as it is on the opposite side of the country, on the coast of the

Gulf of Mexico, though it has a similar climate and soil to Jalisco. The decision followed a request to the Mexican president, José Lopez Portillo, by Tequilera La Gonzaleña in Tamaulipas, which was already producing a "tequila", but not on a commercial basis.

The rights to the name "tequila" were also established as the intellectual property of the Mexican government, with distilleries requiring permission from the authorities to use this term.

For several years following the 1976 NORMAS, a government department also regulated and verified production methods in each tequila distillery. However, as tequila exports continued to expand, the Mexican government decided to transfer responsibility for this function to the private sector. This resulted in the Consejo Regulador del Tequila (Tequila Regulatory Council) being established in 1992. The Consejo Regulador supervises the entire production process in each distillery, and certifies that it complies with the NORMAS. This includes verifying the level of agave or other sugars used, as well as sealing barrels and vats for ageing tequila. The initials CRT on bottle labels therefore indicate that the production has been supervised by the Consejo Regulador del Tequila.

The Consejo Regulador also awards separate licences to distilleries for "standard" tequilas (which include fermentable sugars from sources

Above

Gonzaleña barrels signed, sealed and stamped according to regulation – standards and quality are rigorously monitored by an independent bureau.

other than agave) and the "premium" 100 per cent agave tequila. Many distilleries produce both types.

Tequila bottles carry a NORMA Oficial Mexicana (NOM) number. This identifies each tequila distillery by its official number, which is assigned by the Mexican Secretary of State for Commerce.

Although Mexico has had an agreement with the USA since 1976, under the terms of which both countries respect the denomination of origin of bourbon and tequila, a new era for tequila and mezcal was launched recently when both spirits gained "denomination of origin" status within the EEC. This followed an agreement signed on 27 May 1997 (the result of about 15 years' negotiation between Mexico and the EEC), which provided tequila and mezcal with a legal definition and protection. As part of the agreement Mexico also recognised the denomination of origin status of more than 100 European spirits, including Scotch whisky, Cognac, Armagnac and kirsch.

Besides extending the status of tequila and mezcal beyond the "sombrero and poncho" cliché, Mexican producers were concerned about so-called tequila produced in Spain, Italy, Belgium, Germany and Greece. While some of these Euro-tequilas were based on agave, many brands were simply neutral spirits produced from molasses with added flavourings. Nevertheless, these impostors were so successful that annual sales were estimated to have reached 80-100,000 cases. Retailing at around half the price of genuine tequila, these brands also created consumer confusion, and threatened to undermine tequila's phenomenal growth in Europe. Under the EEC agreement, producers of Euro-tequila were given a year (until May 1998) in which to either discontinue production or market these spirits under another name. The agreement in Spain also allowed producers a further year, until May 1999, in which to continue selling stocks of "tequila" produced before May 1998 – on the proviso that existing production levels were not increased.

South Africa was another source of pseudo-tequila, some of which was even distilled from locally grown agave plants. With annual sales estimated at around 275,000 cases this was obviously a significant market. However, an agreement in 1998, protecting tequila's denomination of origin status, saw production of "local-tequila" banned in South Africa.

Internationally, tequila production is currently in the 10-12 million case a year category, with the USA being the most important export market at around 5 million cases. The American market began to develop in the 1970s when tequila was "discovered" in California and the south-west. Serious interest in super-premium and boutique styles is fuelling further growth in the USA, just as it is in Mexico, which accounts for around 3.5 million cases. Europe accounts for almost 1 million cases, with Germany a key market.

Total annual tequila production in 1997 was 17.4 million cases, which accounted for almost 720 million kg of agave. Production of "standard" tequila increased by almost 8 per cent on 1996, and accounted for just over 72 per cent of the total. The quantity of 100 per cent agave tequila is also developing rapidly. While this sector accounted for only 2 per cent of total tequila production in 1995, it had increased to almost 28 per cent in 1997, and is expected to continue this rapid growth.

There are currently 53 tequila distilleries operating in Mexico, producing a total of approximately 350 brands. (This also includes the production of tequila brands on behalf of other drinks companies.) Rising production levels are particularly evident in the town of Tequila, where the total of 14 distilleries in 1994 rose to 32 in 1998, with most of the town's 20,000 population employed by the tequila industry. There are only two distilleries outside the State of Jalisco: Corralejo, which markets *Reposado* ("rested") and *Añejo* ("aged") tequila under the same name, is located in Penjamo in the state of Guanajuato; and La Gonzaleña in the state of Tamaulipas produces the Chinaco brand. (Tequila Sauza operated a distillery in Tamaulipas until the early 1980s, when all production was transferred to the town of Tequila.)

Increasing specialisation has seen tequila undergo a profound change of image in Mexico, with an enormous growth in interest since the beginning of the 1990s. Whereas tequila was traditionally perceived as being a rustic, as well as the least expensive, spirit, its recently elevated status has seen sales approach the levels of brandy and rum, which have traditionally dominated the Mexican market. And, rather than being served with fruit juices or a mixer, as tequila traditionally was, it is increasingly appreciated neat by Mexicans because it really does offer a range of characteristics to savour. Tequila is also an "equal opportunity" spirit, with as many female as male devotees – in fact, it is particularly Mexican women who are driving the popularity of the Reposado sector.

Moreover, whether at a chic society event or a simple lunch in a cantina, tequila has established itself as Mexico's national drink, and now transcends social and class consciousness. Consequently, the rise of tequila has coincided with the growing sense of a modern Mexican identity, rather than the traditional distinctions of being of either Spanish or Indian descent. Now Mexicans throughout the country are raising glasses of tequila together and repeating *salud!*

The History of José Cuervo

As the world's leading tequila producer, José Cuervo is also the most historic, with Don José Antonio de Cuervo first producing tequila in 1758. He was also the first to begin cultivating agave, on his hacienda the Cofradia de las Animas. This land, on which wild agave originally flourished, was granted to him by the King of Spain, in appreciation of Don José having managed the parish church in the town of Tequila.

In 1795 the deed for this land was transferred by King Carlos IV to Don José's son, Don José Maria Guadalupe Cuervo. He was also granted the first concession to produce tequila commercially, founding the La Rojeña distillery in the same year.

Opposite
La Rojeña – the original Cuervo distillery in the town of Tequila, built on agave land granted to the Cuervo family by the King of Spain.

Don José Maria Guadalupe Cuervo's daughter, Maria Magdalena Ignacia, inherited the distillery. She married Vicente Albino Rojas, who re-named the distillery Fabrica La Rojeña. Rojas promoted the family's tequila not only in the state of Jalisco, but also at fairs and festivals within Mexican states across the country. While the distillery subsequently changed hands several times, it always remained within the ownership of the Cuervo family.

Two figures who influenced Rojas were Jesus Flores and José Cuervo Labastida. In anticipation of tequila's potential sales across Mexico after the arrival of the railway in Tequila, Flores increased the amount of agaves under cultivation, and maximised production levels. He also relocated the business to more functional buildings. Not surprisingly, the railway soon replaced the traditional teams of mules, and gave José Cuervo better access to a far broader Mexican market and to the United States. As already mentioned, José Cuervo's first recorded exports were three barrels of tequila sent to El Paso in Texas in 1873. Another innovation pioneered by Flores was the use of individual bottles for tequila, which had traditionally been sold in small wooden casks. Many Indian customers couldn't read Spanish, but as Cuervo means 'crow' or 'raven,' each barrel was emblazoned with the image of a black bird, which meant that the brand could be ordered simply by pointing at the barrel.

Flores had been married to Ana Gonzalez Rubio and after his death she married José Cuervo Labastida. He was a direct descendant of the family patriarch, and introduced a modern approach to the business, amassing patents and trademarks, not to mention awards. Meanwhile, an ideal way to begin the 20th century was featuring the Cuervo brand-name on each bottle of the company's tequila.

Under José Cuervo's leadership the distillery prospered, with an inventory of about 300 mules and horses, 112 pairs of oxen, and fields planted with around 4 million agave plants. Cuervo tequila also began to develop an international reputation. Not only had they been awarded the medal at the 1889 Paris Exposition, and the so-called 'agave brandy' from Tequila been honoured at the Chicago World Fair in 1893 but Cuervo tequila also won awards at the Madrid Gran Premio of 1907, and the Grand Prix at the International Food & Hygiene Exhibition in Paris in 1909. José Cuervo and his wife Ana also shared their success with the town of Tequila, endowing the hospital, bringing piped water into the area, and renovating municipal and parish schools.

The business subsequently passed into the hands of Guillermo Freytag Schrier and his son Guillermo Freytag Gallardo, followed by Cuervo heirs Juan Beckmann Gallardo and his son Juan Beckmann Vidal, who has taken the company

Right
*An old José
Cuervo fresco at
La Rojeña
distillery. Cuervo
means 'raven'
and barrels of
their tequila
were originally
marked with an
image of the bird
for the many
customers who
couldn't read
Spanish.*

forward in terms of both exports and research and technology. The Beckmann surname first entered the Cuervo family tree when Juan Beckmann's great-grandfather, then Germany's ambassador to Mexico, married a Cuervo daughter. Not all Cuervo descendants have gone into the family business. In the late 19th century

Antonio Gomez Cuervo became provisional governor and military commander of the State of Jalisco. The Cuervo family has also provided other governors, as well as the first Cardinal of Mexico and Archbishop of Guadalajara, not to mention the first Bishop of California.

Cuervo's original distillery, La Rojeña in the town of Tequila, has more recently been joined by another distillery called Los Camichines, located in La Laja in the highlands of Jalisco. La Rojeña, which produces 100 per cent agave tequila, produces daily around 80-100,000 litres of spirit at 55 per cent abv. The Los Camichines distillery operates on a similar scale.

José Cuervo's annual sales are currently around 4.7 million cases, with exports to more than 80 countries. José Cuervo is the top-selling tequila in Mexico, and also the leading brand outside Mexico, with a 40 per cent share of the world's tequila market.

The American drinks company Heublein acquired a 45 per cent shareholding in José Cuervo in 1991. Heublein had been acquired by International Distillers & Vintners, the drinks division of Grand Metropolitan plc, in 1987.

SAUZA HISTORY

The rooster that features in the Sauza corporate logo represents pride, in producing quality tequila, and tradition, with the company dating from 1873. That was when Don Cenobio Sauza established the La Perseverancia distillery in the town of Tequila, on the site of La Antigua Cruz hacienda, the first commercial tequila distillery. Don Cenobio had left his home town of Teocuitalan, Jalisco at the age of 15, to see what opportunities the tequila industry offered, and served his apprenticeship in the San Martin distillery before deciding to set up on his own.

Don Cenobio became renowned as a technical innovator, for example introducing new production methods in the agave fields, and using steam coils rather than direct fire to provide indirect heating of the pot stills.

Don Cenobio's tequila soon achieved international recognition. His son Eladio, born in Tequila in 1883, carried on his father's tradition, taking over the family firm and opening additional offices in Mexico City and Monterey, while another office was also established in Mazatlan, a key point for distribution. Eladio began modernising the distillery by adding new equipment, and also introduced new brands of Sauza tequila.

Don Eladio's son Don Francisco Javier Sauza took over the business in 1931 and, as a guarantee of quality, he decided to include a facsimile of his signature on every bottle, while also broadening distribution. Sauza was the first tequila company to set up an experimental agave farm, Rancho El Indio just outside the town of

Tequila, where research into various growing conditions and clones of the blue agave and many other varieties of agave plants, is on-going.

As international demand for tequila increased in the 1970s, a partnership was formed between Sauza and the leading Mexican brandy producer, Pedro Domecq. This partnership led to Pedro Domecq's complete purchase of Sauza in 1988. In 1994, Pedro Domecq was acquired by the UK conglomerate, Allied Lyons, which resulted in the formation of Allied Domecq, the company's spirits division.

Above

Something to crow about – while Cuervo might have their ravens, the roosters on the Sauza crest signify pride in the product.

43

PRODUCTION

AGAVE CULTIVATION

Growing throughout Central and South America, agave is characterised by a bulb bearing rosettes of slender but incredibly tough leaves, around 1-2 metres long, which have a shimmering combination of blue and green colourings. Despite appearing to resemble a type of cactus, the agave is a "succulent" that belongs to the *agavaceae* family. Agave is also known as maguey in Mexico, a term that originated with the Spanish conquistadors, while the typical American reference is the century plant (because the plant was thought to live for a hundred years).

Mexico has around 200 species of agave. It was first classified as *Agave americana* in 1755 by one of the most renowned naturalists of his time, the Swede Carolus Linnaeus (1707—78), also known as Carl von Linné. Linnaeus had another link with alcohol through his treatise *Vodka in the Hands of a Philosopher, Physician and Commoner*. This was inspired by a gift of Russian vodka from Catherine the Great.

A subsequent, and more appropriate classification was "Mexican agave", courtesy of

the renowned French biologist and botanist, Jean-Baptiste Pierre Antoine de Monet (1744—1829), who was technically the Chevalier de Lamarck. After studying for the priesthood, followed by a stint in medicine, he turned to biology and botany, and pioneered the theory that plants evolve according to their environment. In 1905 a German botanist named Weber embarked on classifying the different varieties of agave, with blue agave subsequently named in his honour: *agave tequilana weber azul*. The word "agave"' is taken from the Greek and literally means "magnificent", "admirable" or "noble", while "azul" refers to the plant's blue leaves.

Blue agave is native to the state of Jalisco. Its combination of climate, altitude and soil make it

Above

The Jalisco landscape is dominated by the "noble" blue agave plant. It is the only region in the world where the plant grows indigenously.

45

the only region in the world where blue agave grows indigenously. It was perfectly logical that blue agave became the sole variety used to produce tequila. It has a larger piña (the 'heart' of the plant) than other varieties. Its piña also contains a higher level of starch, and it is the starch that is vital for distillation. Moreover, compared with other varieties, blue agave contains less fibre and less water, the undesirable but inevitable elements of distillation.

It is possible to grow agave from seed, but no one bothers to as, at around 3 years of age, an agave becomes a "mother" plant, and produces several "baby" plants. Technically classified as rhizomes, these "babies" are referred to in Mexican as *hijuelos*. The mother plant has two root systems: one extends deep into the soil to look for water; the other, which develops just below the surface of the earth, yields the hijuelos. Of the six to nine hijuelos produced annually by each mother plant, only the strongest three or four are selected for replanting. Moreover, hijuelos are usually collected from mother plants up to the age of 6, after which the hijuelos produced are too weak to replant.

The hijuelos are selected by the *jimador*, literally the "harvester", but the jimador also undertakes all aspects of the plants' cultivation. The skill of the jimador is handed down from father to son, and it's not unusual to see three generations working together in the fields.

Opposite

El Jimador – a brand named in honour of the skilled harvesters who tend the agave fields.

Replanting takes place when the hijuelos are about 1 year old, by which time the "bulb" is the size of an orange or grapefruit and the stem is about 50 cm high. The hijuelos are separated from the mother plant using a *barreton*, a traditional tool comprising a long wooden stick with a small blade at the end. All it usually takes is a single slice through the base of the stem, with the hijuelos subsequently trimmed of extraneous leaves and roots using a *machete corto* (small machete). The hijuelos are then left to dry out in the agave fields for about a month (a small reserve of water within the bulb keeps the plant alive during this time). While no one can cite scientific evidence for it, this drying-out period undoubtedly results in stronger growth when the hijuelos are replanted. Moreover, this tradition also reflects the fact that it is impractical to collect and replant hijuelos in the same day. A jimador can remove and trim around 1,000 hijuelos in a typical working day of 6 am– 1 pm, after which the sun is too hot for this type of physical labour.

Hijuelos are collected only in late spring, ready for replanting in April and May. This timing

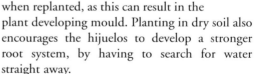

protects them from the relatively cooler winter weather and also ensures that the hijuelos are established before the rainy season of June-September. Other than during the rainy season, when there is a couple of hours' rainfall a day, it is not unusual for there to be a complete absence of rain. The advantage of dry conditions for the jimador is that dry soil is easier to prepare for replanting, which means digging a small hole in the ground for each hijuelos, using either the barreton or a *talache* (small pick-axe). Experience also shows that hijuelos grow better if they are not watered in when replanted, as this can result in the plant developing mould. Planting in dry soil also encourages the hijuelos to develop a stronger root system, by having to search for water straight away.

Planted in rows about 1 or 2 metres apart, for ease of maintenance and harvesting, the bulb of the hijuelos initially develops below the surface of the soil, then, seeking light, the majority of the bulb grows above the surface. The incredibly tough, sword-shaped leaves (called *pencas*) are edged with needles, which protect the plant as it grows. While the plants are still small, some farmers allow cattle, horses and goats to graze between them, an effortless way to weed the

land. However, as the pencas are sharp enough to injure grazing animals, not to mention the jimador, plants are usually pruned at the age of 5, and then again during the year before they are expected to reach maturity. Pruning also strengthens the plant by encouraging a faster growth rate and earlier maturity. However, some farmers say the resulting piña is smaller compared to that of an unpruned plant.

Despite each plant's large number of pencas, a jimador can prune around 2-3,000 plants daily, using a *machete barbeo* ("large machete"). The swashbuckling series of swings inflicted on each plant are actually very economical movements,

Above
The cultivated agave are planted in rows a couple of metres apart for ease of maintenance as the plant's sharp needles can be treacherous.

49

depending entirely on the wrist action rather than swinging the arm.

As agave fields are not irrigated, the plants rely almost exclusively on the rainy season for their water supply, although they do obtain limited amounts of moisture throughout the year from overnight dew. The pencas have a minimal surface area and are wax-coated, both factors preventing water-loss through evaporation. The agave has a great capacity for amassing reserves of water, accounting for up to 95 per cent of the plant's total volume. During severe droughts plants may shrivel, but they soon recover at the start of the rainy season. Irrigation may seem to be an obvious benefit for the plant, and research conducted by José Cuervo showed that watering agave during the dry season did indeed result in larger piñas. However, the additional weight was entirely accounted for by water, there being no increase in the piña's starch content, which is the most important consideration. Consequently, irrigating is simply not worthwhile except for the purely aesthetic benefit of the agave plants taking on a deeper blue colour.

Occasional frosts or even snow cause no lasting

damage, though frost can kill a plant's pencas, which means reduced photosynthesis and thus a temporarily reduced growth rate. However, frost damage is dealt with by pruning away any affected pencas, and encouraging new growth. Similarly, the snow that fell in Jalisco in 1997, the first for around 100 years, lasted only a couple of hours, but this was still long enough to "burn" the pencas of many plants. The snow also killed some hijuelos that were less than a year old.

However, two far more serious and long-term threats to the agave emerged in 1992—3: one is the erguinia bacteria, which attacks the root structure and effectively dries up the plant's sap; the other is a small insect called fusarium, which attacks the pencas. Agave affected by either of these offenders cannot be used to produce tequila. Although research has been on-going since 1995, there is still no effective solution to either problem, which is thought to have affected up to 30 per cent of the total number of agave plants. Moreover, the presence of the bacteria or the insect is impossible to detect until the plant has been infected for 5-6 years.

GROWTH

On average, agave takes 8-10 years to reach maturity, reaching a height of around 1.5 metres. Plants are individually selected by the jimador, as even agaves growing next to each other may reach maturity 2-3 years apart. Plant selection is crucial: if harvested too early, their starch content is too low, and the resulting spirit lacks depth and character. On average, 10 per cent of the plants in the same agave field reach maturity in 7 years, 20 per cent in 8 years, 50 per cent in 9 years, and the balance of 20 per cent requires 10 years.

A state-of-the-art means of keeping an inventory of plants, and monitoring agave fields, is the satellite system used by José Cuervo since 1994. The plants' age can be calculated by their density in the fields, while a satellite is also an effective way of monitoring the fires that can occur because of the arid climate.

Tequila companies are constantly researching how to increase the agaves' rate of maturity and how to make the land more productive. Sauza, for instance, runs an experimental agave field at the El Indio ranch just outside the town of Tequila, researching different growing conditions and various clones of the blue agave. A typical way of improving productivity is to leave the land fallow for a couple of years before replanting with agave. The tradition of growing annual crops, such as corn and beans, among rows of agave, has also largely been discontinued, as it obviously reduces the agave's growth rate. This practice is now limited to small-scale farmers, who plant 'cash crops' to tide them over while waiting for the agave to mature.

Increased maintenance of agave fields is, of course, another positive factor though some agave fields owned by small-scale farmers still receive virtually no maintenance. Its not unusual for such a farmer to plant agave and then spend several years working in the USA before returning to harvest the fields. Agave from an untended field may reach a weight of around only 10-20 kg, compared to the usual 60-100 kg (with a similar starch content, relative to the size of the piña). However, a smaller piña isn't necessarily harder to sell, as it's the degree of maturity rather than the size that counts.

SUPPLY AND DEMAND

Historically, an absence of planning and monitoring the amount of agave under cultivation resulted in a continual cycle of shortage followed by surfeit – with the price of agave fluctuating accordingly. The current surplus of agave is expected to have equalised by the year 2000. Moreover, this is expected to be the last period of surplus, as the Tequila Regulatory Council is working closely with distillers and farmers to plan carefully for future needs.

Many farmers are safeguarded against periods of oversupply by having exclusive contracts with distillers. Not only does this guarantee a supply of agave to the distiller, but they are also able to

Opposite

*Agave is often
supplied by
networks of
small
independent
farmers, who
generally have
long-term
contracts with
tequila distillers.*

exercise greater quality control. José Cuervo, for instance, has contracts with more than 400 farmers.

Contracts between distillers and agave farmers fall into two principal categories: one option enables the farmer effectively to "rent" his land to a distiller, for an all-inclusive annual fee that covers maintenance costs and the eventual price of the agaves; with the other, the farmer can opt to receive a lower annual maintenance fee for the land but receive payment equivalent to 80 per cent of the current market price when the agaves are harvested.

Farmers operating without contracts (which of course means bearing all costs and selling agaves on the open market), may obviously be unable to find a buyer during a surplus period. Such farmers have even been known to blockade distilleries in an attempt to force a sale of their agaves. Far from succeeding, some farmers ended up with a prison sentence.

Meanwhile, in addition to buying agaves from independent farmers, many distillers own agave fields. Historically, tequila companies were not allowed to own agave fields, though it was easy to side-step this regulation: principals of family-owned distilleries simply bought land privately, rather than through the company. Changes to the regulations in 1994 have since allowed tequila companies to own a certain amount of land for cultivating agave, and the trend is towards further liberalisation.

HARVESTING

Selecting and harvesting mature agaves, which means that the starch content has reached a maximum level, is undertaken throughout the year. An obvious sign of maturity in female

plants is the appearance of the *quixotl* ("stalk"), which shoots up from the piña. This stalk, bearing yellow and white flowers containing seeds, can reach a couple of meters. It must be cut off as soon as it appears, otherwise it feeds on the nutrients and sap stored within the piña and reduces the starch content, making the plant unsuitable for tequila production. The appearance of a stalk always contains an element of surprise, as without it even the jimador is unable to determine the gender of an agave plant. Once it is there, we can, of course, all tell.

Harvesting is very demanding work, and in the absence of any suitable machinery everything is done manually by the jimador and his *coa*, a long wooden pole with an oval-shaped, razor-sharp blade at one end. The coa was introduced about a hundred years ago, replacing a cumbersome and less efficient tool resembling a pick-axe. The jimador initially removes the plant's wax-coated pencas, a process known as *jima* (Nahuatl Indian for "harvest"). The pencas are a hindrance to the distilling process, so it is considered a great skill to remove them as close to the surface of the piña

as possible. It takes just a few minutes to strip away the pencas, with a jimador typically working his way through 3-5 tons of piñas daily, which necessitates sharpening the coa every couple of hours. Pencas are subsequently recycled by being ploughed back into the soil as fertiliser. The coa is also used to slice the piña from its root system and, once separated, the piña is simply rolled over with the foot.

It takes approximately 7 kgs of piñas to produce 1 litre of 100 per cent agave tequila. A piña typically weighs 60-100 kgs. The term "piña" stems from the Spanish for "pineapple', which fruit it resembles, though in a giant size. The piña can also be referred to as a *cabeza* ("head").

Above
Harvesting is still the preserve of manual labour. The jimador uses his "coa" to strip away the leaves as close to the piña as possible.

57

In addition to the tools of the trade, two other essential accessories are carried by a jimador. One is a small supply of lard, kept in a goat's, cow's or bull's horn clipped to the jimador's belt. Regular applications of this lard prevent blisters. And, as harvesting is thirsty work, the other extra is a hollowed-out, dried gourd to carry water, an efficient (and historic) method of keeping it cool.

TERROIR

While the concept of "terroir" – the influence of the soil and individual microclimates – is mainly used in relation to fine wine, the principle also applies to tequila. Wine connoisseurs may scoff at this, but the tequila region incorporates different soils and microclimates, which can have a significant effect on the piña.

Jalisco, for example, comprises two principal regions for agave cultivation: the lowlands, including the towns of Tequila, Amatitan and El Arenal; and the highlands (referred to as Los Altos), including Arandas, Zapotl, Gonzaleña, Tepatitlan and Jesus Maria. Commercial agave cultivation in the lowlands, particularly around the town of Tequila, dates from the 18th century whereas agave was first cultivated commercially in the highlands during the mid-19th century, but only in significant amounts since the late 19th century. While the highlands region is still

dominated by small- and medium-scale farming, the lowlands are largely the preserve of large-scale farming. Nevertheless, the highlands have made up for lost time: approximately 120 million agave plants are currently under cultivation in the highlands, compared to around 67 million in the lowlands.

Climatic differences between the two regions are minimal, with temperatures marginally hotter in the lowlands (an average of 18-25°C) than the highlands. This is hardly surprising as the town of Tequila is at an altitude of 1,000 meters above sea level, while Atotonilco is at 1,500 meters and Arandas at 2,000 meters. While it is slightly windier and cloudier in the highlands, the level of rainfall is similar in both regions, totalling around 800 mm per year.

A more obvious point of differentiation is the soil. Lowlands soil is volcanic, whereas the

Above
The vibrant red soil of the Jalisco highlands is rich with iron resulting in a higher starch content in the piña and a finer end product than that derived from it's lowland cousin.

vibrantly red brown soil of the highlands reflects its far higher iron content. Many distillers claim the iron content as the reason why highland agave offers a higher level of starch compared to lowland agave (which makes it the most expensive on the market). Highland agave is also said to be softer than lowland, so it requires less cooking time. However, the average age of maturity in the highlands is 9 years, compared to 8 in the lowlands.

Another difference between the two regions is that the lowlands optimum yield is obtained from a density of around 4,000 plants per hectare, compared to the highlands average of around 3,500 per hectare. An exception to this is the highlands producer Tres Magueyes, with around 2,750-3,000 plants per hectare. This is due to the spacing between the rows of agave plants being unusually wide, at around 3.25 meters (compared to the usual 1-2 meters), while also allowing 1.2 meters (rather than 1 meter) between each plant. The rationale is that increased space allows more light to reach the plants, resulting in a higher rate of photosynthesis and growth, not to mention a higher level of soil nutrients for each plant. Although other growers initially expressed disbelief that such a system could result in any advantages (Tres Magueyes has used this system for the past 12 years), the results are larger piñas harvested at around 7 years of age, each of which are individually selected by the company's founder, Don Julio Gonzalez. Despite the lower number of plants per hectare, Don Julio says this system is not more expensive to operate, as the advantages of harvesting larger piñas that mature more quickly balance out the additional investment required.

While it is tempting to compare the merits of tequila produced from highland agave versus lowland agave, evaluating the two regions on this basis is difficult. While there are some tequilas produced exclusively from highland agave, such as Tres Magueyes and El Tesoro de don Felipe, many distillers in the lowlands also use highlands agave. Similarly, some highland producers also use lowlands' agave. Moreover, the agave is only one element that influences the final tequila, and how a distiller utilises the agave is ultimately more important than its source.

COOKING THE PIÑA

On their arrival at the distillery, the piñas are unloaded from large trucks in the shade (to keep them in optimum condition). They are immediately halved or quartered, generally with an axe though some distilleries are equipped with electric saws, to prepare them for cooking. The objective is to obtain standard sizes to ensure a uniform cooking time. Cooking the piñas converts their high levels of starch into

Below

The piñas,
weighing
60-100 kg, are
loaded manually
into the ovens.

fermentable sugars, chiefly fructose (fructosa in the vernacular). Cooking also caramelises other types of sugars within the piña, which influences the eventual flavour of the tequila. A more practical consideration is that cooking softens the piña's tough fibres, which makes milling far easier (the next step in the production process).

The traditional cooking vessel is either an adobe, stone or brick oven. Adobe is the most traditional oven, made from a combination of mud and either straw or agave fibres, and is renowned for the ability to retain heat. However, an adobe oven must be protected from rain, either by being under a roof or, more typically, by having a brick shell built around it. Herradura is among the few producers to retain brick-enclosed adobe ovens, with 24 hours of cooking followed by a 24-hour cooling period. To prevent any heat from escaping, the edges of the oven doors are "sealed" in the traditional manner with moist agave pulp.

Stone and brick ovens are also a time-consuming option, while arranging the piñas by hand, is an exercise that in itself takes several hours. At Centinela, for instance, the piñas bake for 36 hours in a stone oven (which has walls three feet thick), followed by a further 36 hours in the oven without any additional heat and the oven doors closed. The cooking process is even more leisurely at Tequila Tapatio, extending to 48 hours' cooking time, followed by 24 hours with the heat turned off and oven doors closed.

The modern alternative to these ovens is the autoclave, a vast stainless steel vat, which cooks the piñas under pressure (typically at around 1 kg per square cm) in a minimum of 12 hours. The choice of autoclaves is either the horizontal type or the much larger vertical. Sauza has used giant

vertical autoclaves for the past 20 years, with the piñas mechanically fed into the top of the autoclave, having been shredded to ensure even cooking on the way up. Each batch takes about 14 hours to cook. The piñas in both types of autoclave are subsequently allowed to cool for several hours before unloading.

Needless to say, distillers speak in favour of their own cooking method. Traditionalists believe that slower cooking, followed by equally slow cooling, yields piñas with a higher level of sugar and a lower level of methanol; and consequently a finer and more characterful spirit. They also claim that an autoclave does not always cook the agave quite as thoroughly as an oven, which means that not all the starch is converted into sugar. Another opinion is that ovens and autoclaves yield the same level of sugar from the piña, though ovens lend a better flavour. In favour of the autoclave, producers say it is a more efficient process than using an oven, with a far shorter cooking time. Some producers use more than one type of cooking vessel: at La Arandina, for instance, autoclaves are used in conjunction with brick and stone ovens. According to the company, the autoclave is the most efficient, though brick and stone ovens produce sweeter piñas (due to slower cooking). And while stone ovens produce the same result as brick ovens, stone ovens retain heat better so are less expensive to run, but are initially more expensive to build. Take your pick !

Opposite
Herradura is one
of the few
producers to
continue using
the traditional
adobe oven.

65

Whichever type of oven is used, the piñas are steam-cooked. The steam, released into the oven by a series of pipes for uniform heat distribution, is generally produced using spring water from the distiller's own well. An important consideration is to safeguard against overcooking, as this caramelises the piñas and reduces the level of fermentable sugars. Overcooked piñas can also have a caramelised flavour. Seasonal adjustments to the cooking time are another factor: the piñas can be very dry during the summer, which necessitates extra cooking time as the piñas must initially be rehydrated; in winter they tend to have a higher level of moisture and thus slightly softer fibres, which reduces the cooking time. As the piña comprises about 40 per cent fibre, the level of moisture has a significant effect.

MILLING

Once the piñas have cooled, the sugars are extracted by crushing the pulp and stringy fibres, usually by modern milling methods. Only a couple of producers still use the traditional *tahona*.

Tequila Tapatio's L'Altena distillery in the highlands, which produces El Tesoro de Don Felipe, still uses a tahona. The distillery has two milling sessions daily. Each session takes about 90 minutes to process around 4 tons of piñas that have initially been chopped with a pick-axe into

smaller pieces. The wheel is a single piece of stone weighing around 4 $\frac{1}{2}$ tons, and has served the company since 1937. Maintenance is minimal, the grooves on the surface of the wheel being rebored every 2-3 years. The wheel is pulled around the pit by a small tractor (a slight concession to modernity), with a labourer in the pit constantly shovelling piñas into the path of the wheel. Once the piñas are crushed, the agave juice and fibres are manually transferred, in wooden buckets carried on the workers' heads, from the pit to wooden fermentation tanks. Using a tahona is at least three times slower than using modern milling equipment, not to mention the estimated 5-6 per cent wastage, but these disadvantages are still outweighed by the end result, according to the

Above

A traditional tahona mill is rarely used as most distillers now use hi-tech milling equipment for this part of the process.

company. But Tequila Tapatio is also experimenting with modern mechanical milling, to see how the tequila is affected by different milling methods. How much longer the tahona remains in active service there remains to be seen.

The Seagram distillery in Arandas is also researching with a tahona, exclusively for 100 per cent agave tequila. This is a tahona with a slight difference, as two large pneumatic wheels fitted with an integral engine are attached to the stone wheel and the pole in the centre of the tahona. The wheels cruise around the perimeter of the tahona, taking the stone wheel around the stone-lined pit.

Modern milling methods mechanically shred the piñas, while jets of cold water wash the sugars from the pulp, yielding *mosto* or *aguamiel* ("honey water"). The volume of water used during the milling process, as well as the level of sugar within the resulting mosto, is constantly monitored. Using too little water during milling means that not all the sugars are being extracted from the fibres: using too much yields a "thin" liquid in which the sugar content is too low through excessive dilution. It might seem that using hot water in extracting the sugars would be more efficient than cold water, though in fact hot water could result in the sugars being reabsorbed by the agave fibres.

Milling obviously produces vast amounts of waste pulp, referred to as either *bagazo* or *marrana*. Research to find profitable ways of recycling waste pulp is on-going. In the meantime the pulp is usually given away for free to the collector. It is subsequently used in a variety of ways: as cattle feed, fertiliser for agave fields, stuffing for upholstery and car seats, and protective packaging for pottery and other handicrafts, and to produce a parchment-style paper. The pulp can also be combined with mud to produce the traditional adobe bricks to build houses.

FERMENTATION

The fermentation process used depends on the type of tequila being produced: either standard tequila or 100 per cent agave tequila. For 100 per cent agave tequila all the sugars during the fermentation process must be derived from agave. Although 100 per cent agave tequila requires a greater initial investment, it is more profitable than standard tequila.

For standard tequila, a minimum of 51 per cent of the fermentable sugars must be derived from agave, with the balance accounted for by any other type of sugar (regulations do not limit the choice). Typically this is either molasses, *piloncillo* (unrefined and crystallised sugar cane juice produced in Mexico), muscovado (unrefined brown sugar) or corn syrup. Each offers a slightly different aroma and flavour, which can be evident in the resulting spirit.

Above
Massive stainless steel fermentation tanks are a practical part of the modern process.

The choice of sugar depends on the distiller's own particular style. The neutrality of molasses and corn syrup is an attraction for some distillers, while the more pronounced flavours of muscovado and piloncillo are considered an asset by others. Piloncillo, a favourite of numerous distillers, is produced in Veracruz and St Luis Potosi. It arrives at the distillery shaped into small cones, which are dissolved in hot spring water before being added to the fermentation tanks. Some producers also combine different sugars, with La Arandina, for instance, blending piloncillo with unrefined white sugar to prevent the piloncillo flavour being too dominant.

Using additional sugars enables the distiller to use fewer piñas, and so reduce production costs. Some producers exceed the 51 per cent minimum, either because they prefer a stronger agave flavour or because they are helping to use up the current oversupply of agave. While this may be a case of paternalism, distillers are, of course, also taking advantage of lower prices. La Arandina, for example, is currently producing standard tequila that contains 80 per cent agave, which will be reduced once the oversupply ends.

As well as sugars, some producers add the *miel de los hornos*, meaning "oven honey" or "oven syrup". As the name suggests, this liquid is steam that has condensed and combined with juices released by the piñas, which drains along special channels in the oven floor. Generally the oven syrup from the first few hours' cooking is discarded, as at this stage its sugar content is too low and also contains bitter notes from traces of wax from the stubs of the pencas. Only the "middle batch"' of oven syrup, which has a sugar content of around 12-15 per cent, is actually used in tequila production. This is collected after several hours cooking, and for the remainder of the cooking period. Oven syrup collected once the heat is turned off is not used. Some producers use oven syrup in both their standard and 100 per cent agave tequilas.

Fermentation tanks are now nearly always stainless steel, the consensus being that there is no difference in the end result between stainless steel and the traditional wood. Stainless steel also offers the practical advantage of being much easier to clean.

The traditional practise of fermenting the mosto together with agave pulp is now limited to a few distillers, such as Tequila Tapatio. At the company's L'Altena distillery, agave pulp accounts for about 30 per cent of the total volume – within the equally traditional fermentation tanks made from Mexican pine. According to the distillery, fermenting in wood gives a better result than stainless steel, on the basis that wood is porous and allows carbon dioxide and oxygen to pass through the sides of the tank. Moreover, a sufficiently high level of oxidation occurs to yield a more complex tequila.

Fermentation was traditionally effected entirely by natural airborne yeasts, with nothing being added to the mosto. This approach is now very rarely used, though one exponent is Tres Mujeres, with the company claiming a fuller agave flavour as a result.

Most distillers add their own secret strain of yeast, which is generally obtained from cooked piñas, though a minority also prepare yeast from oven honey collected during the cooking process. Other options, used by a very few companies, include using commercially prepared yeast or adding fermented mosto from a previous batch (similar to the "sour mash" method used to produce Bourbon). Selecting which type of yeast to use is a very important consideration. As the amount of yeast accounts for around 5-10 per cent of the total volume within the fermentation tank, it obviously has a significant effect on the end result. Moreover, adding yeast not only reduces the length of the fermentation period, but also gives the distiller more control over the entire process. Distillers tend to use the same strain of yeast whether preparing blended or 100 per cent agave tequila.

Fermentation tanks are typically left open. The length of fermentation can vary enormously between producers: while the typical time-scale is 48-72 hours, it can also extend to several days. At Tres Mujeres the "'yeast-free" fermentation lasts 4-5 days. Just as many producers claim that cooking the piñas slowly results in a better result, so some say that slower fermentation results in a more complex flavour. Mosto with added sugars (for standard tequila) obviously requires less time to ferment than 100 per cent agave mosto.

An unusual extra has been added to the fermentation process at Cazadores, with the company claiming to have discovered the secret of how to reduce fermentation time without resorting to artificial additives. The

Below
Traditional fermentation vessels made from Mexican pine at the Herradura distillery museum.

average fermentation period at this distillery is now 8 days – which represents an improvement of approximately 15 per cent on the previous time-scale. Guess what! It's all due to the classical music that fills the air from a CD player installed in the fermentation area. The selection of 40 recordings, which play day and night, includes Bach string concertos and Mozart. Soothing classical music is best, says the company. I suggested they try playing mariachi music, which might accelerate the process even further.

Once fermentation is complete, the mosto, now referred to as *mosto muerto* ("dead must") has an alcoholic strength of between 5 and 10 per cent abv, and is ready for distillation. It takes a lot of mosto muerto to produce even a small amount of tequila, with the figures at La Cofradia, for instance, being 18,000 litres of mosto muerto resulting in approximately 1,800 litres of tequila spirit at 55 per cent abv.

DISTILLATION

Distillation is a straightforward process, based on the fact that alcohol boils at a lower temperature than water. Therefore, heating a fermented liquid within an enclosed container, drawing off the alcoholic vapours, then cooling and condensing the vapours, will yield alcoholic spirit.

Tequila is double distilled using pot stills, the

most historic method of distillation, also used to produce other spirits such as Cognac and malt whisky. The pot still, effectively a circular kettle, has remained virtually unchanged since the Dutch invented this process in the 16th century. Vapours rise into the neck of the still and are conducted along a condenser (a coiled pipe cooled by water), which condenses the liquid.

Pot stills were originally made of copper. While a number of tequila distilleries still use copper pot stills, stainless steel is now the norm. Some distillers claim that copper yields a superior result, on the premise that copper helps to eliminate volatile sulphurous compounds. Others, though, say that using either copper or stainless steel makes no difference to the quality of the resulting spirit. Moreover, stainless steel is frequently preferred on the basis of simple economics: copper stills are around four times more expensive than stainless steel. Another practical consideration cited is that stainless steel offers less risk of contamination by being easier to clean than copper.

The first distillation, known as *destrozado* or *estozaminto* (meaning "breaker" or "broken up") produces spirit at around 25 per cent abv, which is known as *ordinario*. This usually takes between 90 minutes and 2 hours. Only the "heart" or "middle cut" is used from each batch, with the inferior spirit at the start and finish of each batch, known as "heads" and "tails", being redistilled. The second distillation yields much

Right
The traditional copper pot still is believed by some to reduce volatile sulphurous compounds.

stronger spirit, typically at 55 per cent abv. Distilling to a higher strength obviously takes longer, typically around 3-4 hours. The strength at which the spirit is distilled has an important influence on the eventual character, as the higher the strength, the more impurities are removed. However, this purity is also achieved at the expense of losing flavour and character. The distiller therefore aims to balance purity with flavour and character, drawn from the raw material.

If double distillation yields a better-quality spirit than single distillation, then why not go for a third time as well? The answer is that distilling twice generally produces the best results, with the potential result of a third distillation being a thoroughly "laundered", neutral spirit. Triple distilling is, however, used successfully by Porfidio to produce limited quantities of Plata, an unaged style. The three-stage distillation goes up to 28 per cent, 37 and 50 per cent abv respectively, resulting in an ultra-smooth and soft agave character.

L'Altena distillery is virtually unique in retaining traditional distillation methods, by which the first distillation is based on mosto muerto together with agave pulp. Wooden fermentation tanks are manually emptied by a labourer standing inside the tank, filling wooden buckets with mosto muerto and agave pulp, which are carried (on the head) to a copper pot still. The still is fitted with a large "spout", which makes it easier to empty the buckets – still balanced on the head.

There are isolated uses of continuous stills being used for the first distillation process. As the name suggests, this type of still facilitates a continuous process of distillation, unlike pot stills which can only distil spirit in batches. The continuous still dates from 1831, when it was devised by Aeneas Coffey, an Irish exciseman. The advantages of using a continuous still are cited as speed and economy, without compromising the end result. This type of still is far more expensive to construct than a pot still,

Above
Both economical and easy to clean, stainless steel is now favoured by most for the distillation process.

but it is also faster and more economical to operate, without compromising the end result. The heart of the continuous still is a cylindrical column containing a number of plates that jut out across the interior. Steam enters the base of the column, the mosto muerto is fed into the top, and they bounce back and forth across the plates in a process which separates the alcoholic vapours. These are captured and cooled in a condenser. In contrast to the pot still method, the strength of the final spirit can be more accurately controlled: the more plates the still contains the greater the opportunity for the spirit to distil, and the stronger the result. It can take as little as 10-15 minutes to produce spirit at a strength of 60 per cent abv, prior to a second distillation in a pot still at 55 per cent abv.

After distillation, each batch of new tequila spirit is traditionally tasted from a hollow bull's horn by the master distiller, a ritual that is maintained by only a few distilleries. Production levels vary enormously throughout the industry, with independent specialists such as Tres Mujeres producing 2,000 litres a day, compared to a large-scale distillery at around 80,000 litres daily.

MATURATION

The strength at which tequila is aged, the type of barrel used and the length of the ageing period all have an important influence on the end result. Regulations concerning the ageing process, which is supervised and certified by the CRT, stipulate that only oak barrels are used for ageing, while the parameters for ageing and bottling tequila are between 38-55 per cent abv. A practical, not to mention financial, consideration is that fewer barrels and consequently less space are required by ageing tequila at 55 per cent abv, rather than 40 per cent abv. Distillers who prefer to age their product at the top end of this scale include José Cuervo and Sauza, who age tequila at 55 per cent abv before bringing it down to bottling strength by diluting with demineralised water. Other distillers stick to the other end of the scale in order to avoid diluting their tequila prior to bottling, their philosophy being not to "add" anything after distillation. For this reason La Arandina sets the second distillation at 38.5 per cent abv, which is also the strength the tequila enters the barrels, and evaporation during the ageing process adjusts the strength to around 38.2 per cent abv, the brand's bottling strength. A similar approach at Tequila Tapatio's L'Altena distillery sees the second distillation and ageing at 40 per cent abv.

Tequila gains a significant amount of flavour and aroma, not to mention colour, from wood ageing. The typical choice is barrels previously used to age Bourbon. These are charred on the inside – a tradition that originated in Kentucky during the late 18th century. Exactly how it started is unclear, though the Reverend Elijah Craig, a Baptist preacher, generally gets the credit. As well as being a preacher, he was an entrepreneur and the founder of Georgetown. It was perhaps his Scottish nationality that led him to begin distilling whisky in Kentucky in 1789. Apparently a cooper working for him was heating strips of wood into curved staves and accidentally charred one over the fire. The stave was nevertheless used to make up a barrel (the minister was also known to have been very frugal). The whiskey stored in this barrel was deemed to have a mellower, superior flavour. It was one of those fortunate mistakes that have resulted in a great tradition - which tequila has also benefited from.

Bourbon barrels are widely considered to result in the smoothest tequila, while also enhancing the agave flavour. Another characteristic of Bourbon barrels is that they colour the spirit more quickly than uncharred (or "new") barrels. Despite the long tradition of using Bourbon barrels, producers are increasingly using and experimenting with other types of barrels. One alternative is to use charred American oak barrels that haven't already been used to age bourbon, this type of barrel being one of the reasons why Porfidio Reposado develops such spicy characteristics. Using new (uncharred) oak imparts a more dominant wood flavour, a prime example being Barrique de Ponciano Porfidio.

Below
José Cuervo ages its tequila in the barrel at 55 per cent abv diluting it to bottling strength after maturation.

This is aged for a minimum of one year in new French limousin oak casks. Being medium-grained and porous, Limousin oak is renowned for developing fine wines and Cognac with strength and balance. Moreover, casks used for Barrique de Ponciano have a capacity of 100 litres, which accounts for an intensity reminiscent of Cognac, as well as subtle oak flavours.

Cazadores is testing a 50/50 blend of tequila using new American white oak barrels in conjunction with ex-Bourbon barrels, with new French oak also being assessed, possibly to produce an Añejo style. Tequilas del Señor is taking a similar route, blending tequila aged in new white American oak barrels with tequila aged in ex-Bourbon barrels, to yield what the company says is a superior result.

Barrels previously used to age sherry are also used by Tequilas del Señor to produce a "special edition" Añejo tequila. This tequila is aged for 12 months in a 500 litre ex-sherry barrel, from which 75 litres are removed once a year and replaced with 75 litres of Reposado, which then spends a year in the barrel before being drawn off and replaced by another 75 litres of Reposado; and so on. The tequila drawn off is marketed as Diligencias Aged Tequila.

Centinela's experiments with ex-Scotch whisky barrels led to the conclusion that the influence of the wood was too dominant, while ex-Cognac barrels were also considered inappropriate for the

house style. On the other hand, ageing in ex-Cognac barrels is an important element of El Tesoro de Don Felipe Paradiso, a super-premium style launched in 1998 by Tequila Tapatio. The ageing process incorporates 2 years in ex-Bourbon barrels, followed by 2 years in ex-Cognac barrels, with a final year in large oak vats to further refine the flavour.

Single barrel tequila is another option, rather than the standard practice of blending from various barrels. The appeal for connoisseurs is that no two barrels of tequila will ever be quite the same. Porfidio produces a single barrel Añejo (known as "Cactus"), aged in new, medium-charred 200 litre American oak barrels. These barrels are used only once, with ageing usually between 1 and 3 years, depending on how long each barrel takes to reach its peak.

Opposite
The original
fermentation
tanks set into the
floor at the
Herradura
distillery
museum.

Tequila is almost always aged in warehouses at ground level, with temperature not really an issue as the temperature in Jalisco remains fairly constant at around 18-25°C throughout the year. One brand that is aged in an underground cellar, at the company's distillery in the town of Tequila, is José Cuervo Reserva de la Familia. Production of this super-premium style (matured in new oak barrels) is limited to around 80,000 bottles per annum. Centinela constructed an underground cellar in 1998, which is initially being used to gauge the effect of "cellar conditions" on a 3-year-old style. Meanwhile, Centinela's main ground-level ageing area comprises the original adobe walls, which means local earth, water and agave fibres mixed together by treading, then baked into bricks.

Wherever tequila is stored, evaporation is of course an issue. At La Gonzaleña for instance, a Reposado matured at 55 per cent abv for 11 months results in evaporation of around 12 per cent in terms of volume, which consequently lowers the alcoholic strength to 51-52 per cent abv. Another consideration is how different types of barrels affect the rate of evaporation. A new oak barrel containing 100 litres of tequila would evaporate off around 5 litres of alcohol in a year, which compares to around 10 litres from an equivalent ex-Bourbon barrel.

STYLES OF TEQUILA

Tequila is graded according to the level of agave it contains, in addition to the length of ageing, both of which result in various styles with individual characteristics.

Blanco (also known as "silver") is the original style, and means unaged tequila. Some companies bottle blanco almost immediately after distillation. Others incorporate a "resting" period prior to bottling, which refines the flavours by enabling them to "marry". Sauza Blanco, for instance, rests in stainless steel tanks for a couple of weeks, while Tapatio Blanco rests for almost a month in white oak vats (the maximum resting period permitted is up to 30 days).

Joven abocado tequila has certain characteristics that imply wood ageing, such as a golden colour, but this is derived entirely from permitted additives such as caramel (produced from either sugar or corn). Current regulations limit the addition of caramel or sugar-based syrup to 1 per cent of the total weight of the tequila.

Authentically aged styles are marketed as Reposado and Añejo, with ageing a relatively recent development in the tequila industry, dating from the 1950s. Reposado was the first aged style, an innovation popularly attributed to Don Julio Gonzalez, the founder of Tres Magueyes. Añejo was a logical progression following the success of Reposado. Caramel can be added to adjust the colour of both styles.

Reposado receives between 2 and 11 months in oak vats or barrels (with no restrictions on the size of barrel or vat used). For bulk sales, Reposado is typically aged in 19,000 litre-capacity vats called *pipones*. Both standard tequila and 100 per cent agave tequila are aged to produce Reposado.

Añejo receives a minimum of one year in oak barrels with a maximum capacity of 600 litres. However, 180-200 litre barrels are the norm (the smaller the barrel, the greater the influence of the wood). Añejo tends to be produced from 100 per cent agave rather than standard tequila.

Producers are increasingly experimenting with longer ageing, resulting in brands such as Don Julio Real, a blend of 3- and 5-year-old tequilas, while José Cuervo's Reserva de la Familia and El Tesoro de Don Felipe Paradiso each receive 5 years' ageing. The inevitable question is: how much ageing potential does tequila actually offer? Despite the growing demand for ever more premium styles, the consensus is that producers have already reached the limit with 5 years ageing. Beyond this tequila can easily lose its essential agave character and begin to resemble a generic whisky or brandy. Moreover, the influence of the wood becomes too dominant and lends the tequila an unpalatable bitterness. Another practical issue is that after 5 years' ageing, evaporation could account for up to 50 per cent of the barrel. This means that, even if

Opposite
*As with whiskey,
the type of barrel
used during
maturation is
crucial to the
end result. Ex-
Bourbon has
traditionally
been most
favoured.*

longer ageing succeeded on the palate, it would be a very expensive exercise.

RELATIVE MERITS

Our love of superlatives naturally dictates that 100 per cent agave styles, with maximum barrel ageing, automatically lead the tequila hierarchy. However, tequila's agave character can be so robust and overpowering that "diluting" it with other sugars can be an advantage. It all depends, of course, on personal taste. Moreover, each style of tequila has its own individual merits.

Blanco is upheld for offering the freshest, most intense agave flavour. This can range from a straightforward combination of herbaceous, earthy aromas and flavours to more complex styles, offering a wonderful spiciness embracing cinnamon and pepper as well as vegetal notes and even a hint of marzipan in the follow through.

Reposado and Añejo combine agave characteristics with the influence of wood ageing. This can, however, result in ultra-smooth (and ultimately unfulfilling) styles, dominated by vanilla and caramel, with the agave character only occasionally surfacing (if you're lucky). But Reposado and Añejo can also be a revelation, where the influence of the wood underpins the essential agave character, providing aromas that span perfectly judged amounts of the inevitable

caramel and vanilla, together with nutmeg, set honey and the earthy spiciness of agave. On the palate, luscious flavours can reveal a range of caramel, vanilla and dark chocolate richness, cooked fruits, burnt oranges, earthy, peppery, spicy hints like cinnamon, nutmeg and gingerbread, and varying degrees of smokiness that incorporate capsicum peppers among chargrilled vegetal flavours. Fabulous!

Ultimately, of course, the finest tequila is the one you like – whatever its credentials.

MEZCAL, SOTOL AND PULQUE

Although tequila has established a far more international profile than mezcal, tequila is actually a type of mezcal, which is a generic term for agave spirit. The name "mezcal" is derived from the Nahutal Indian word, meaning "roast agave". However, mezcal has individual characteristics that distinguish it from tequila, reflecting a difference in the varieties of agave used and the production methods. Mezcal generally has a more powerful and smokier nose than tequila, and is more pungently earthy, spicy and herbaceous on the palate.

While mezcal is indigenous to various regions, the state of Oaxaca in southern Mexico is renowned for producing some of the finest examples. The Zapotec and Mixtec Indians

living in Oaxaca have traditionally cultivated specific varieties of agave, from which they originally collected the sap to produce pulque. The majority of Oaxaca distilleries are still run by Zapotec Indians. Moreover, Oaxaca, which covers the municipalities of Zimatlan, Sola de Vega, Tlacolula, Ocotlan, Ejutla, Miahuatlan and Yautepec, gained Denomination of Origin status in 1997. Mezcal is also produced throughout central Mexico, including in Jalisco, as well as in Acapulco, Guerrero, Zacotecas, St Luis Potosi and Durango.

Above
Peddling refreshment – the majority of mezcal distilleries are still run by the indigenous Zapotec Indians.

91

Mezcal production totalled around 10 million litres in 1997, up from 8.5 million litres the previous year. While production is expanding rapidly, it is still a fraction of tequila's level. There are only a few international brand owners, such as Monte Alban and Gusano Rojo, and around half a dozen medium-sized, family-owned companies. Consequently, production is still centred on numerous small-scale distilleries and regional brands, with some villages even having their own exclusive brands.

As the industry evolves, some independent producers are combining their resources into larger co-operatives. The Asociación de Magueyeros de Oaxaca, for instance, was formed in 1990, grouping together various small-scale mezcal producers from the village of Matatlan, which has a long tradition of cultivating agave. Mezcal producers are also co-funding a Consejo Regulador (Regulatory Council), following the lead of the tequila industry, to regulate and certify the production process in each distillery. This follows the formation of a Mezcal Chamber at the beginning of the 1990s, which acts as a political negotiating body.

CULTIVATION

As with blue agave, hijuelos aged between 6 months and 1 year are taken from mother plants, with 3 years considered the optimum age for a mother plant. All aspects of the plants' cultivation are undertaken by campesinos, who plant hijuelos just before the rainy season, which in Oaxaca is May to September, while further south it usually runs from August to October. Agaves are not irrigated, and any shrivelling suffered by the plant is soon remedied by the first downpour of the rainy season.

Mezcal producers typically have contracts with independent farmers to ensure a consistent supply of maguey, but increasingly producers are also acquiring their own agave fields. Agave is typically grown in conjunction with other crops such as corn and beans, providing farmers with an annual income while waiting for the agave to mature. This results in an average of 1-2,000 plants per hectare, and a maximum of 2,500-3,000 plants per hectare when agave is cultivated without any other crops. The comparable figure for tequila is 4,000 plants per hectare.

Several species of agave are used to produce mezcal, including tepestate, larga, and wild varieties such as silvestre and tobala. From the 25 varieties of agave growing in Oaxaca, the Denomination of Origin regulations include the following varieties: de cerro, de mezcal, tobala, verde o mezcalero and espadin.

Whether in Oaxaca or other regions, the most popular variety is espadin (technically Agave angustifolia Haw, popularly known as the "blue variety"). Espadin has a larger piña and higher level of starch than other varieties of agave used

Opposite
Mezcal's distinct
characteristics
stem from the
local species of
agave grown in
Oaxaca's rich
volcanic soils as
well as different
production
methods.

to produce mezcal. While many producers, including Mezcal Monte Alban, use only espadin, and its widespread cultivation is partly based on tradition, long-term studies into production with other varieties of agave are also being undertaken.

Oaxaca is renowned for its temperate climate and rich volcanic soils, with experience showing that espadin grown on hillsides and at higher altitudes matures faster, and develops a higher starch content, compared to espadin grown on level land at lower altitudes. Espadin grown in this more advantageous location also yields mezcal with more flavour and aroma. Consequently, up to 80 per cent of Mezcal Monte Alban's agave plants are cultivated on hillsides, using specially created terraces about 1 metre high, which are deep enough to absorb more water than level land. These agaves reach maturity at around 8 years, compared to 10-12 years on flat and low-lying land. Plants are pruned at 2-3 years of age, which means removing the top 20 cm of the pencas, to encourage stronger growth.

PRODUCTION

The traditional cooking method is still used by many producers. This means a stone-lined "oven" dug into the earth to a depth of 4-5 meters. The oven is typically filled with dense Mexican woods, either huizache, tepehuaje or

Above
Monte Alban –
one of the first
mezcal brands to
reach the
international
market.

encino, which burns for about a day and heats the underlying rocks. Once the fire has been reduced to embers, the piñas (brought to the oven using mules) are placed on the embers. The final layer of piñas is covered by a layer of pencas, earth and usually a waterproof ground-sheet woven from agave fibres. Cooking takes 2-3 days and is supervised by a *practico*. As the cooking process determines the nuances of aroma and flavour, as well as the smoothness of the resulting mezcal, the appropriate degree of cooking is vital. Thus the skill and experience of the practico is to take into account variables in the piñas and climate, and to ensure that they are neither undercooked nor overcooked.

Once cooked, the piñas are removed from the pit, chopped up and crushed, usually using a tahona though an alternative is beating the piñas with wooden mallets. Subsequently the agave juice and fibres are fermented together, with added water usually accounting for 10 per cent of the total volume. In some instances the piñas are crushed using a modern milling line, and the sugars washed from the agave pulp using jets of water. Most producers do not use yeast to effect fermentation, which can take anything from several days to 4 weeks, yielding a liquid known as tepache. The agave fibres that rise to the top of the fermentation tank (buoyed up by carbon dioxide) are known as the "sombrero".

A mezcal distillery is referred to as a *palenque*, and the distiller or owner is the *mezcalero*. Traditionally mezcal was single distilled, though double distillation in pot stills is now the norm. The stills are usually made of copper, though ceramic is a historic alternative. Many producers retain the agave pulp within the fermented mosto for the first distillation. This traditional practice is said to result in a higher level of methanol, which is why producers such as Licores Veracruz distil mezcal three times. Using copper pot stills, the first distillation is at 22-26 per cent abv, and the second 43-46 per cent abv, before diluting the spirit to around 25 per cent abv with demineralised water and distilling a third time at 46-50 per cent abv. Diluting the spirit produces a better result and retains the agave flavour more effectively. The higher the strength of distillation the greater the degree of purity achieved, but at the expense of flavour, and producers agree that beyond 65 per cent abv the spirit starts to loose agave flavours.

Filtration through cellulose and charcoal softens the aroma, while filtering through sand also refines the flavour, texture and clarity. Regulations stipulate that mezcal can be bottled between 36 per cent and 55 per cent abv.

Mezcal is typically 100 per cent agave, though the regulations also allow standard mezcal, which contains up to 20 per cent of fermentable sugars derived from sources other than agave, usually piloncillo. Labelling regulations due to be introduced in 1999 will follow the same principles as for tequila, with 100 per cent agave mezcal indicating this on the label. Currently mezcal brands do not indicate the level of agave. The label also indicates whether the mezcal was bottled at the distillery (envasado de origen) or elsewhere in Mexico (envasado en Mexico).

Mezcal is also graded according to the degree of ageing. Blanco, the traditional style of mezcal, is unaged: joven is also unaged but acquires the characteristics of ageing through the addition of caramel. Tobala is an unaged style of mezcal, named after the variety of wild agave from which it is produced. Mezcal con gusano (with the worm) is usually bottled a month after distillation.

The practice of ageing mezcal dates from the 1950s, with producers using either new white oak, evergreen oak, or ex-Bourbon barrels (which are charred on the inside). Reposado (also referred to as madurado) is matured for between 2 and 11 months: Añejo (also referred to as anejado) is aged for a minimum of one year, in barrels with a maximum capacity of 200 litres. It is also permitted to add caramel to adjust the colour of both aged styles.

Experiments with longer ageing are on-going though, as with tequila, 5 years is considered to be the limit. But just to prove there are always exceptions, Ultramarine emerges triumphantly after 6 years of wood ageing. Its charcoal nose leads to luscious caramel and vanilla flavours laced with smokiness, with a chargrilled aftertaste.

Mezcal liqueurs, flavoured with chilli peppers (mezcal con chilli) or with oranges (crema de mezcal), are also produced. Mezcal is usually drunk straight up, particularly as an aperitif, accompanied by *botanas*, Mexican hors d'oeuvres. Blanco accounts for only a small segment of the Mexican market, with this style most popular in northern Mexico, particularly in rural areas. Meanwhile, about 95 per cent of mezcal sales are accounted for by Reposado, a trend largely fuelled by urban bohemians and professionals.

As the mezcal market matures, it is expected to polarise with standard brands comprising blended mezcal, and 100 per cent agave accounting for the premium sector (although aged styles can be made from blended or 100 per cent agave mezcal).

GUSANO

Despite mezcal's numerous merits, it has always been most notable for containing a worm in each bottle, which is the practice in Oaxaca. One school of thought suggests the tradition stems from Aztec priests adding a worm to pulque – a symbolic way of endowing the drink with a spirit of its own. Another possible explanation is entirely practical: historically, spirits were often adulterated by innkeepers and sold below their usual strength (increasing profit margins considerably). However, a bottle containing a worm preserved by alcohol was proof that the mezcal was at an appropriate strength. Having served this practical purpose, the worm takes on a different role. It is washed down with the last glass from the bottle as part of a macho ritual.

Nevertheless, consuming a worm is believed to be far more than just a show of machismo. Some claim that the worm induces a spirit of celebration or that it imparts strength (both benefits that could equally be attributed to the mezcal consumed in the course of emptying the bottle). Taking those two factors a step further is the worm's reputation as an aphrodisiac – which may stem from its suggestive shape. Then again, just as the Aztecs used pulque containing a worm in a religious context, the worm is also said to be like a "medium", leading the spirit to a mystical world beyond.

Whether the worm actually adds flavour to the mezcal is open to speculation. Some producers claim the worm's "unique" quality (well, it would have to be "unique", wouldn't it?) adds a certain sweetness to the flavour and aroma, as well as colouring the spirit. The vital statistic quoted in support of this claim is the worm's protein content, which is around 80 per cent (with the balance accounted for by fat). Other producers

say the worm's contribution to the aroma and flavour is absolutely zero.

Even if the worm is incapable of imparting anything to the mezcal, it undoubtedly offers flavour in itself. A favourite accompaniment to a glass of mezcal is a condiment of roasted worm ground with salt and chilli and served with fresh lime. Indeed, the worm enjoys gourmet status (as do grasshoppers and other insects) in Oaxaca, where it is typically enhanced by a complement of green tomato and chilli sauce, served within a taco (a favourite dish dating from the Aztecs). Nor is the appeal of the worm limited to rustic venues – it is served in even the most exclusive restaurants.

Moreover, referring to this creature as a worm simply doesn't do it justice. Mexican terms such

Above
Mezcal drinking has long been a ritualised part of the macho culture.

101

as *gusano*, *gusano rojo* (red worm) or *gusano de maguey*, (worm of the agave plant) sound far better, even if they mean the same thing. However, the gusano is actually the larvae of the Mexican mariposa night butterfly. This petite species (around 3 cm in length and 5 mm wide) has brown wings and, true to its name, flies only at night – a combination of factors which makes it very difficult to see.

The mariposa lays its eggs (*mansos*) on the pencas of agave plants, as close to the piña as possible because the developing larvae head straight for the piña, which they feed on. Only young agaves are selected by the mariposa, as the piña has much softer fibres than a mature plant so the larva is able to consume more of the piña, and more easily. Consequently, including a gusano in a bottle of mezcal is an ironic way of continuing the relationship between the two, and a nice way for the plant to get its own back.

Gusanos are collected in the south of Mexico at the beginning of the rainy season, when they leave the piñas to form a chrysalis. There is no such thing as a "gusano industry"; it's simply a case of local people collecting gusanos and selling them privately. However, things aren't what they used to be, and distillers are concerned by the declining numbers and escalating price of gusanos. Meanwhile, distillers are researching ways of safeguarding the gusano population, with studies on-going at Veracruz University.

Otherwise the bleak news is that the gusano could become extinct within 5 to 10 years. On average its life-cycle is one year.

One note of hope is that not all premium mezcals include a worm. Whether this is an ecological move is open to speculation, though its also clear that the presence of the gusano isn't always considered appropriate in a premium brand. Moreover, the gusano is not collected solely from the maguey de pulque, but also from a wild variety called Maguey arruqueno tobala, which is not used for mezcal production. The variety of agave from which the gusano is collected doesn't ultimately make any difference.

Mezcal Monte Alban, the world's top selling mezcal among gusano-containing brands, is safeguarding its supply by collecting gusanos from the company's own ranch. The method entails raising the piñas of 2-3-year-old plants slightly above the soil but without actually extracting them from the ground or severing the roots. Once the base of the piña is exposed, the surface is prised open with the fingers to remove between 50 and 70 gusanos from each piña. The plant is subsequently repositioned and continues growing quite happily, relieved of all trespassers. A certain number of these gusanos are transferred to young agave plants to provide the next generation. The remainder are cooked in stainless steel containers, then rinsed and stored in mezcal for about a year. This allows enough time to remove the surface grease from the gusano, which ensures that it sinks to the bottom of the bottle, rather than floating around.

SOTOL: THE SPIRIT OF CHIHUAHUA

This traditional speciality of Chihuahua is rarely seen in any other part of Mexico. The Tarahumara and Apache Indians of the Chihuahua region originally fermented agave sap to use in religious ceremonies, with distillation introduced by the Spanish conquistadors.

Sotol is produced from a specific variety of agave called *Agavacea dasylirion Wheeleri*, more commonly called the sotol plant. This wild variety grows in the mountains of the Chihuahua desert, between the pine forests of the Sierra Madre and the desert's high plains. Consequently, it grows at higher (and colder) altitudes than agave cultivated for tequila or mezcal. An extensive conservation program is in place to ensure the continued availability of the sotol plant in its natural habitat.

On average, sotol takes at least 10 years to reach maturity, compared to 8 years for agave in Jalisco. Moreover, the sotol's piña weighs approximately two-thirds less than an average blue agave piña (usually 60-100 kg), with around 14 kg of sotol piñas needed to produce a litre of spirit, about twice the necessary weight of blue agave. Unlike tequila, which can include up to 49 per cent of its fermentable sugars from other sources, sotol can be produced only from

100 per cent agave sugars. A Denomination of Origin status, similar to that which protects tequila and mezcal produced in Oaxaca, is being sought by sotol producers.

Sotol is aged in oak barrels, using the same terminology for aged styles as tequila and mezcal (Reposado and Añejo). Sotol is generally drier than tequila, with the wild terrain in which the plant grows adding a more intensely earthy flavour.

Among the leading sotol producers is Vinomex, a subsidiary of a major real estate company, with a distillery located in Delicias, south of the town of Chihuahua. Vinomex distils the Hacienda de Chihuahua brand, which is currently being distributed internationally.

PULQUE

Having been around for at least 2,000 years, pulque has continued as a Mexican speciality. However, even as an inexpensive alcoholic drink, at around 5-8 per cent abv, its popularity is waning. Pulque is drunk neat or *curado* (flavoured with fruit juice). Even its traditional reputation as an aphrodisiac, and (allegedly) endowing great strength, can't halt its decline. Pulque traditionally enjoyed its own specific venue, a *pulqueria* – an inexpensive neighbourhood bar with a pretty wild atmosphere. There are still pulquerias in Mexico City – though it has only been since the end of the Second World War that men and women have been allowed to mix inside these establishments.

BRAND DIRECTORY

TEQUILAS

ALTENO

Reposado, 100 per cent agave, 40 per cent abv. Deep, pungent but clean and focused aromas, light on the palate with a definite vegetal edge plus vanilla and caramel sweetness.

LA ARANDINA

Dating from 1938, the distillery is in Arandas in the highlands of Jalisco, and only uses highlands' grown agave from the company's own fields.

Casco Viejo joven, 38 per cent abv.

Tahona joven, 100 per cent agave, 38 per cent abv. Very mellow agave nose, subtle hint of caramel with a light spicy agave flavour, very gentle with minimal heat.

La Arandina Reposado, 100 per cent agave, 38 per cent abv. Aged 4 months.

Amigos Reposado, 38 per cent abv. Aged 4 months.

Cava de Don Agustin Reserva Reposado, 100 per cent agave, 38 per cent abv. Aged 8 months in new white oak Canadian barrels. Perky on the palate with a lovely hint of caramel sweetness supporting an elegant, up-front agave flavour. Elegant style with a rich earthy note.

ARETTE

Reposado, 100 per cent agave, 40 per cent abv. Lightly smoky nose with hidden touches of caramel that dominate as the bouquet opens up. Ultra-smooth palate with touches of set honey sweetness, plus a shot of caramel, with agave opening up in the follow-through.

ARRIBA

Marketed by the German drinks company Dethleffsen International. Both styles available have a small bottle in the form of a green cactus, which can subsequently be used as a salt cellar.

Silver (blanco) and Gold (Reposado), both 38 per cent abv.

CASA SIETE LEGUAS

Located in Atotonilco in the highlands of Jalisco. Blanco, 100 per cent agave, 40 per cent abv. Vegetal nose with earthy overtones, quite subtle on the palate with a full-bodied core that comes through with a strong vegetal base, cinnamon and deep, set honey sweetness together with root vegetable overtones. Lingering nutmeg finish with set honey notes.

Reposado, 100 per cent agave, 38 per cent abv. Very light colour with only glints of gold. Agave nose opens up with a generous amount of caramel and vanilla, a smooth combination of agave and caramel on the palate, with an edge of honeyed sweetness and gentle heat.

D'Antano de la Casa Añejo, 100 per cent agave, 38 per cent abv. Agave nose laced with caramel, on the palate agave combines with caramel and a tingle of cinnamon. Rounded, elegant palate but full-bodied with pepperiness, and a dry finish that encourages the next glass.

CASTA

Añejo, 100 per cent agave, 40 per cent abv. Quite a closed nose with a hint of agave, while a mild agave flavour melds with luscious caramel, providing a straightforward combination with light peppery heat build-up. Hand-made "artisan" bottle with a green glass agave plant at the base.

CAZADORES

Established in 1973 in Arandas, initially producing for private consumption only, and a commercial enterprise since 1982. Currently only one style is produced, though experiments with Añejo are on-going.

Reposado, 100 per cent agave, 38 per cent abv. Aged 2 months. Clean agave nose with hints of

vanilla and caramel. Elegant earthy, spicy, pungent agave flavours supported by subtle hints of vanilla and caramel. Impressive and full-bodied.

CENTINELA

Centinela, which means "sentinel", was established in 1896 in Arandas, in the highlands of Jalisco. This traditional family-owned

distillery produces limited quantities of tequila using only highlands' agave, aged in 200 litre ex-Bourbon barrels.

Centinela blanco, 100 per cent agave, 38 per cent abv. Quite a sharp, set honey nose, with light vanilla hints. Ultra-smooth taste with acacia honey, lightly smoky roasted pepper and chargrilled hints, which open out into a full-bodied palate with peppery notes. Short, set honey finish.

Centinela Reposado, 100 per cent agave, 40 per cent abv. Aged in American white oak barrels for 6-9 months. Light, elegant nose with a lovely earthy, lightly peppery pungency on the palate, and a subtle touch of oak.

Centinela Añejo, 100 per cent agave, 40 per cent abv. Aged 12-18 months. Subtle ginger and vanilla on the nose, with earthy, vanilla flavours.

Centinela Tres Anos, 100 per cent agave, 40 per cent abv. Aged 3 years. Rich and elegant on the palate, with hints of vanilla, caramel and nutmeg, balanced by agave herbaceousness.

Caracol Joven 100 per cent agave, 38 per cent abv.

Chimayo, 100 per cent agave. Aged 6 months in French oak barrels. Light, smooth, softly oaky flavour.

CHINACO

Chinaco is the name given to the *haciendados* (owners of large haciendas), who were the patriotic defenders of Mexico during the instabilities and insurrections of the 18th and 19th century. In fact the La Gonzaleña distillery is owned by the Gonzalez family, who are descended from General Manuel Gonzalez, President of Mexico 1880—84. La Gonzaleña is the only distillery in the state of Tamaulipas, with the company extending its holding of agave fields to ensure self-sufficiency by the Millennium (currently agave is also bought in from the highlands of Jalisco).

Blanco, 100 per cent agave, 40 per cent abv. Very spicy nose, with pear, quince and lime hints. Light, clean vanilla, pepper and agave flavours that really open up with cinnamon and vegetal overtones.

Reposado, 100 per cent agave, 40 per cent abv. Aged 9-11 months in 185 litre oak barrels. Hints

Chinaco
The name evokes
the patriotism of
Mexican
landowners
during the
country's
turbulent past.

of peach, apple and quince on the nose, with clean, fresh flavours embracing spices and fruit.

Añejo, 100 per cent agave, 40 per cent abv. Aged 2 $^1/_2$ years in 185-litre oak barrels. Vanilla and caramel nose, followed by a buttery, lightly creamy, caramel palate with vanilla coming through mid-way. Smooth finish.

LA COFRADIA

The company produces around 15 brands, with a further 20 distilled on behalf of other companies, including the De los Dorados range. In 1996 La Cofradia introduced folklore-style packaging, using Mexican handicrafts, produced in Tlaquepaque, a bohemian district of Guadalajara.

Tres Alegres Compadres, each at 40 per cent abv, available in silver, joven, and Reposado, 100 per cent agave. Aged 4 months in white oak barrels.

Edicion Iguanas Reposado, 100 per cent agave, 40 per cent abv. Aged 6 months in white oak barrels. Wonderfully packaged tequila in a ceramic crock with a couple of iguanas perched on the bottle neck.

EL CONQUISTADOR

Blanco, 100 per cent agave, 46 per cent abv. Mellow, marzipan nose, light on the palate, especially considering the strength, with some earthy, green pepper and chargrilled flavours and a perky, peppery quality, with a sweetish cinnamon follow-through.

Reposado, 100 per cent agave, 40 per cent abv. Aged 7 months minimum. Vanilla aromas, followed by rich, smooth citrus flavours.

Añejo, 100 per cent agave, 38 per cent abv. Aged 18 months minimum. Pungent agave nose with caramel hints, palate combines agave and lightly honeyed caramel flavours, with agave opening up in the follow-through.

CORALLEJO

This is the only tequila distillery in the state of Guanajuato, dating from 1755, when it was established by Major Pedro Sanchez de Tagle. Two styles are produced, using Spanish white oak and encino, as well as French limousin oak barrels for ageing. The distillery is open to visitors.

Reposado, 100 per cent agave, 40 per cent abv. Aged 2 months minimum. Lovely vegetal/agave nose with a light pungency. Light caramel, a honeyed sweetness and deep agave notes balance nicely on the palate, together with a hint of chargrilled capsicum, chocolate and cooked orange flavours, and an ultra-smooth gentle heat build up. This style is available in a 1 litre size, bottled in pale green glass, and a 3 litre size in a stunning Bristol blue glass, which the company says sells extremely well in Mexico.

Añejo. 100 per cent agave, 40 per cent abv. Aged 15 months.

JOSÉ CUERVO

The world's largest-selling tequila brand, produced at La Rojeña distillery, established in 1795 in the town of Tequila (for history see pages 36-41).

Blanco, 38 per cent abv. Smooth, clean, distinctive agave flavours.

Tradicional blanco, 100 per cent agave, 38 per cent abv. Thriving on clear, earthy, spicy flavours, this was the company's first 100 per cent agave brand. Packaged in the traditional bottle shape for tequila (half litre size).

Especial Reposado, 38 per cent abv. Aged 6 months. Sweet, caramel and vanilla nose, very smooth on the palate with underlying earthy, vegetal notes.

1800 Añejo, 38 per cent abv. A blend of Añejo tequila with other Cuervo tequilas, aged in ex-Bourbon barrels. Deep vanilla nose with a hint of caramel, exceptionally smooth, rich flavour with vanilla and caramel flavours accompanying agave.

Reserva de la Familia, 100 per cent agave, 40 per cent abv. Launched in 1995 to mark the 200th anniversary of the company, with production limited to 83,000 bottles per annum. Aged 5 years in new oak barrels in a separate underground cellar at La Rojeña distillery. Elegant agave bouquet includes a large dose of vanilla and caramel, with a subtle agave flavour and light lusciousness, followed by a second wave of deeper agave flavour and a caramel follow-through. A wooden presentation case features a graphic design by a different Mexican artist each year.

GRAN CENTENARIO

Produced at the Los Camichines distillery in the highlands of Jalisco, owned by José Cuervo.

Plata (blanco), 100 per cent agave, 38 per cent abv. Deep, evocative agave bouquet, initially subtle on the palate before opening up into a perky, cinnamon, peppery mouthful.

Reposado, 100 per cent agave, 38 per cent abv.

Aged 6 months minimum in new white oak barrels. Pungent vanilla nose, smooth on the palate with vanilla and caramel notes, balanced by a delicious vegetal earthiness and underpinned by a spirited tingle that comes through as part of a distinguished after-taste.

Añejo, 100 per cent agave, 40 per cent abv.

121

HERRADURA

Founded in 1870 on the site of a clandestine distillery. Herradura means "horseshoe", a traditional symbol of good luck. This distillery is one of the most beautiful, having been built around a historic hacienda that now showcases early 20th-century life, together with Mexican handicrafts and art. A museum within the oldest section of the distillery includes a tahona, original fermentation tanks set into the floor, copper pot stills, Mexican white oak barrels (which are very rare), and even a section of the aqueduct which originally supplied water from Jala, 65 km away. All Herradura tequila is produced using agave from the lowlands of Jalisco, including the valley of

Amatitan, which was originally covered in volcanic lava. A combination of Kentucky barrels, charred but unused, and French white oak are used for ageing.

Herradura blanco, 100 per cent agave, 40 per cent abv. Nice herbaceous, grassy, lightly earthy nose, quite spicy on the palate with cinnamon, nutmeg, capsicum and peppery notes, with a lovely molten fluidity and marzipan follow-through.

Herradura Suave blanco, 100 per cent agave, 40 per cent abv. Pungent, slightly peppery nose, very smooth on the palate with subtle though lively agave flavours, attractively garnished with spice, and a clean, fresh follow-through.

Herradura Gold Reposado, 100 per cent agave, 40 per cent abv. Spicy nose and light, elegant, vanilla, caramel flavours with a slowly emerging heat.

Herradura Reposado Antiguo, 100 per cent agave, 38 per cent abv. Aged 11 months. Initially mild agave aroma subsequently joined by vanilla and caramel, though agave maintains its presence. On the palate agave melds nicely with honeyed caramel, lightly luscious vanilla and gingerbread hints, with light touches of cinnamon and nutmeg. Well balanced, as agave is always there, ultra-smooth with gentle heat.

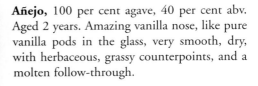

Añejo, 100 per cent agave, 40 per cent abv. Aged 2 years. Amazing vanilla nose, like pure vanilla pods in the glass, very smooth, dry, with herbaceous, grassy counterpoints, and a molten follow-through.

Seleccion Suprema Añejo, 100 per cent agave, 40 per cent abv. Powerful oaky, vanilla nose, with dominant vanilla and caramel flavours bearing dark chocolate hints and gentle heat.

El Jimador blanco, 100 per cent agave, 40 per cent abv. Meaning "the harvester", this brand was launched by Herradura in 1992.

El Jimador Reposado, 100 per cent agave, 40 per cent abv. Aged 3 months in white American and French oak casks. Delightfully smooth, with a balance of agave and the refinements of oak ageing.

MONTEZUMA

Blanco, 40 per cent abv. Smooth, spirited, with some vibrant herbaceous notes.

Gold, 40 per cent abv. A light though complex balance, with a finish that unites herbs and smokiness.

1921

Aged single barrel, 40 per cent abv. With only limited production, this has a lovely, clear agave pungency on the nose with a real sense of the desert. Ultra-smooth on the palate with initial agave flavour supplemented by a burst of caramel and vanilla, balanced by engaging dryness. Focused flavours and a nice molten follow-through.

ORENDAIN

Established in 1926 by Don Eduardo Orendain, who purchased a small distillery known as El Llanito, although the Orendain family had been involved in the tequila industry since 1840. Currently, the company produces tequila at the La Mexicana distillery, in the town of Tequila.

Blanco, 40 per cent abv. Deep, earthy agave nose, smooth and light on the palate, with a silky texture and mellow agave flavour featuring peppery, lightly earthy notes, and a nice light finish.

Extra Joven, 40 per cent abv. Smooth aroma with an elegant serving of agave, accompanied by toffee and caramel hints. Initially low-key on the palate with toffee, fudge and caramel notes, before a mild agave flavour emerges.

Ollitas Reposado, 100 per cent agave. Vanilla

nose with some peppery overtones, rich and delicious palate but still dry blend of vanilla, caramel and perky spiciness.

Reposado, 100 per cent agave, 40 per cent abv. Clean, earthy, pungent agave aroma. Ultra-smooth on the palate, with a mellow, lightly vegetal character garnished with peppercorns, accompanied by a hint of caramel and oaky notes.

Anniversario, 40 per cent abv. Quite spicy, whiskey-like nose with caramel hints. Quite subtle and elegant on the palate, with a lovely alcoholic tingle and whiskey-like warmth. Light caramel and agave hints with deeper oaky notes, with an oaky aftertaste that incorporates a Bourbon-like sweetness.

PATRON
Silver (blanco), 100 per cent agave, 40 per cent abv. Smooth, herby, vegetal nose, ultra-smooth on the palate and a hint of vanilla sweetness.

Añejo, 100 per cent agave. 40 per cent abv. Caramel, vanilla and agave notes are integrated, before agave moves to the fore as the nose opens up. Ultra-smooth on the palate with vanilla and caramel registering before the agave emerges mid-way. Lovely dry and lightly oaky follow-through, which develops an attractive smokiness.

PORFIDIO

This innovative super-premium line was created by Martin Grassl. Far from being Mexican, he was born in 1967 in Austria, where he learned all about distillation at his aunt's eaux-de-vie distillery. He served an "apprenticeship" in the trade by working summer shifts while finishing his studies. Working for an Austrian drinks company that gave him a research project on how to market tequila, he spent a year in Jalisco studying agave cultivation and production techniques at various distilleries, as well as glass factories, while also examining sales and marketing techniques. He subsequently set up his own company and, within a few years, Martin Grassl had achieved cult status for the Porfidio range, comprising specialist brands produced in limited quantities. The company opened a new distillery in Puerto Vallarta, Jalisco in 1998.

Plata (blanco), 100 per cent agave, 40 per cent abv. Triple distilled. Spicy, smoky aroma with a hint of caramelised vegetables. Lightly peppery on the palate, with smooth vanilla and cinnamon flavours that are lightly honeyed, while gentle heat builds up beautifully with a hint of cooked plums, oranges and set honey.

Reposado, 100 per cent agave, 40 per cent abv. Spicy, fresh agave nose, with smooth layers of vanilla, chocolate and oaky flavours, with a deeper vegetal counterbalance on a tingling, warming base. Packaged in an impressive round stoneware bottle with a porcelain finish and 18 carat gold lettering.

Añejo, 100 per cent agave, 40 per cent abv. Aged 2-3 years in ex-Bourbon barrels. Lovely degree of vanilla on the nose, which repeats on the palate balanced by a good degree of pungency, with hints of white pepper, anise and spices within a soft, silky, mellow texture.

Barrique de Ponciano, 100 per cent agave, 40 per cent abv. Limited edition. Aged 1 year minimum in 100-litre (small) French limousin oak casks. Smooth agave nose extends with caramel and Cognac notes, before vanilla element kicks in. Elegant, smooth, clear agave flavour with hints of caramel, honey and chocolate, nice heat build-up with a lush but dry caramel and vanilla finish. Packaged in specially commissioned artisan glass bottles featuring a glass cactus on the base.

Porfidio Single Barrel Añejo, 100 per cent agave, 40 per cent abv. Aged 1-3 years in new, medium-toasted 200-litre American oak barrels that are used only once. The ageing period is determined on an individual basis, according to when each barrel reaches its peak. Warm agave nose laced with vanilla. Ultra-smooth on the palate, though full-bodied and rounded, with the subtlety of an aged Cognac. Creamy, floral, butterscotch and tropical fruit notes.

PUEBLO VIEJO
Reposado, 100 per cent agave, 40 per cent abv. Nicely balanced nose with agave and caramel seamlessly integrated. On the palate it needs a moment to open up before yielding a rounded and fully-integrated mouthful of agave and caramel, with a light capsicum, cooked fruit, cinnamon and nutmeg finish.

PUNTE VIEJO
Reposado 100 per cent agave, 38 per cent abv. Pungent agave nose, spirited, with light vanilla/caramel hints that open up. A central agave flavour is laced with caramelised, chargrilled vegetal notes accompanied by vanilla and nutmeg.

PURASANGRE
Reposado, 100 per cent agave, 38 per cent abv. Smooth agave nose with subtle caramel on the horizon. Ultra-smooth palate, mellow with a rich caramel overtone and light white chocolate notes, nice build-up of heat that accentuates the

agave with chargrilled hints and a molten quality. Rich, sweet finish.

Añejo Gran Reserva, 100 per cent agave, 40 per cent abv. Very light nose with vanilla and caramel hints. Agave is more pronounced on the palate, laced with luscious, lightly honeyed caramel, burnt oranges and gingerbread flavours. A nice molten heat builds up into a gentle grilling. Not ultra-smooth but the degree of character more than compensates for this.

REAL HACIENDA

Reposado, 100 per cent agave, 40 per cent abv. Light vanilla nose with an elegant palate and an earthy pungency, underpinned by vanilla and caramel flavours, and a nice follow-through.

Añejo, 100 per cent agave, 40 per cent abv. Intense caramel nose that repeats on the palate with the accompaniment of sherbet notes.

SAUZA

La Perseverancia distillery, established in the town of Tequila in 1873 by Don Cenobio Sauza (for history see pages 41-43) produces a wide range of leading brands.

Blanco, 38 per cent abv. Hint of earthiness on the nose, lightly earthy, chewy and oaky with focused flavours.

Extra, 38 per cent abv. Aged in white oak barrels. Spicy, herbaceous, vanilla and caramel nose, very smooth on the palate with a subtle pungency.

Hornitos Reposado, 100 per cent agave, 40 per cent abv. Hornitos means "little ovens", referring to the piñas being baked rather than steamed. Deep vanilla nose balanced by pungent agave. On the palate an ultra-smooth smokiness melds with vanilla, caramel and minty notes, balanced by molten vegetal and earthy, peppery flavours, and a tingling warm finish.

La Perseverancia Reposado, 100 per cent agave, 38 per cent abv. Aged 6 months in oak barrels.

Galardon Gran Reposado, 100 per cent agave, 40 per cent abv. Aged 11 months in 200-litre oak barrels. Galardon means "the highest prize", which is appropriate for this complex, perfectly balanced tequila, with soft toasted oak complementing silky agave flavours. Delicate, warm finish.

Conmemorativo Añejo, 100 per cent agave, 40 per cent abv. Aged 3 years. Rich, elegant agave nose with vanilla and raisin hints, smooth agave laced with subtle caramel, peach and cooked fruit flavours on the palate, and a good counterbalance of earthiness, pungency and a molten finish.

Tres Generaciones, 100 per cent agave, 38 per cent abv. Aged 3 years. The agave aromas are wonderfully focused with floral hints. Concentrated on the palate with a controlled degree of richness balanced by a hint of pepper, butterscotch and oak, with a dry, lingering finish of pure agave.

Triada, 100 per cent agave, 40 per cent abv.

The name refers to the Aztec myth of a fusion of fire, air and water. Aged 14 months. The aroma embraces earthy, lightly fruity, agave notes, with a fresh earthiness and gentle heat on the palate that includes toasted almonds and oak, mingled with mild spice, dried fruits and clear agave flavours. Sustained spicy finish.

SEAGRAM DE MEXICO

A local subsidiary of the multinational drinks company, producing two brands at a distillery opened in 1996 in Arandas in the highlands of Jalisco. Only agave from the Arandas region is used.

Mariachi blanco and joven, both 40 per cent abv.

Olmeca blanco and Añejo, both 40 per cent abv. Aged 1 year in ex-Bourbon barrels.

SUAVE PATRIA

Reposado, 100 per cent agave, 40 per cent abv. Very engaging spicy nose laced with caramel, vanilla, cinnamon and light earthiness. Lovely ripe, honeyed, caramel sweetness on the palate, though balanced by dryness with vanilla, gingerbread hints and a light earthiness. Great balance, builds up and opens up nicely with gentle heat.

Tequila del Señor

Founded in Guadalajara in 1943, the Rio de Plata distillery produces a wide range of tequila and tequila liqueur brands, including Herencia de Plata, Rio de Plata, Sombrero Negro, Garcia and Diligencias.

Reserva del Señor Reposado, 38 per cent and 40 per cent abv. Aged 6 months minimum.

Reserva del Señor Añejo, 100 per cent agave, 40 per cent abv. Aged 18 months minimum. Rich caramel nose with vanilla hints, caramel dominates the palate with an underlying hint of agave that slowly opens up and comes through more clearly in the follow-through.

Tequila Tapatio

The company's distillery, L'Altena, uses agave only cultivated in its own fields located in Arandas and the neighbouring municipalities of St Jesus Maria and Adyotlan in the highlands of Jalisco. Production methods are entirely traditional, if not

antique, making it the equivalent of a working museum.

Tapatio blanco, 100 per cent agave 38 per cent abv.

Tapatio Reposado, 100 per cent agave, 38 per cent abv. Aged 3-4 months.

Tapatio Añejo, 100 per cent agave, 38 per cent abv. Deep, clear, lightly earthy agave nose, followed by a lovely dry though rich agave flavour, with gently spicy hints that meld into a richer caramel flavour.

El Tesoro silver, 100 per cent agave, 40 per cent abv. Spicy, tobacco nose, subtle on the palate with rounded agave flavours, a gentle smokiness and subtle liquorice, cinnamon fruity finish, and an elegantly oily follow-through.

El Tesoro de Don Felipe Reposado, 100 per cent agave, 40 per cent abv. Aged 6-9 months. Nice agave aroma with light vanilla and caramel hints. Smooth, warming agave flavour, with a spicy, cinnamon tingle on the tip of the tongue, and a hint of cloves and cooked fruit in the follow-through.

El Tesoro de Don Felipe Añejo, 100 per cent agave, 40 per cent abv. A blend of 2-3-year-old tequilas aged in ex-Bourbon barrels. Very deep agave nose, supported by caramel and vanilla notes; elegant and distinctive. Smooth on the palate, with lightly peppery, deeply earthy, vegetal, fruity notes, with hints of cinnamon and gingerbread. The finish includes a lovely earthy tingle.

El Tesoro de Don Felipe Paradiso, 100 per cent agave, 40 per cent abv. Launched in 1998, with annual production limited to 30,000 bottles, this superlative tequila is aged for a total of 5 years, comprising 2 years in ex-Bourbon barrels followed by 2 years in ex-Cognac barrels, with a final year in large oak vats to mellow the flavour still further.

The sophisticated bouquet is reminiscent of Cognac, with agave hints, together with a caramel and vanilla oakiness. Fantastically smooth, with vanilla and caramel suspended in a luscious mouthful, from which agave emerges in an elegant format. Lovely molten heat and a real smoothie, elegant but medium-bodied. Excellent digestif.

TORADA

Blanco, 38 per cent abv. Herbaceous, earthy nose, with lightly vegetal, herbaceous flavours and a subtle sweetness, with vivid underlying alcohol.

Añejo, 100 per cent agave, 40 per cent abv. Ultra-smooth nose with agave at the heart, and a smooth palate that is a lovely combination of agave with vanilla and caramel, comprising chargrilled, spicy hints, chocolate and nutmeg, with a good build-up of heat. Great agave follow-through with real character, in spite of the smoothness.

TRES MAGUEYES

Established in 1942 by Don Julio Gonzalez, who served his apprenticeship at an uncle's tequila distillery. Don Julio is widely credited for having introduced the concept of ageing tequila, first marketing a Reposado in the 1950s. He still personally selects all the agaves exclusively from fields in the highlands of Jalisco.

Tres Magueyes blanco, 38 per cent abv. Smooth, distinguished, fresh agave character.

Tres Magueyes Reposado, 38 per cent abv. Engaging, subtle agave nose. Beautifully smooth on the palate, with agave character balanced by caramel hints, and a gentle heat build-up. Elegant and silky texture with a good follow-through.

Don Julio blanco, 100 per cent agave, 38 per cent abv. Robust cinnamon, vanilla and nutmeg nose. Ultra-smooth on the palate with a certain lusciousness, peppery with a delicate smokiness and a honeyed, chargrilled sweetness that remains beautifully balanced with a nice degree of heat.

Don Julio Reposado, 100 per cent agave, 38 per cent abv. Aged 8 months. Controlled agave aromas with subtle hints of caramel and vanilla that unfold to a delicious degree. Silky smooth with a compelling combination of light cinnamon, honey and herbaceous flavours balanced by lightly smoky, dark chocolate notes. A certain lusciousness is balanced by a dry finish.

Reserva de Don Julio Añejo, 100 per cent agave, 38 per cent abv. Aged for more than a year in Kentucky oak casks. Fine spicy, peppery agave characteristics linger on the palate. Bottles are hand-blown by craftsmen in Guadalajara, and feature a cap made from Chechen wood, a tree native to Mexico.

Don Julio Real, 100 per cent agave, 40 per cent abv. A blend of 3- and 5-year-old tequilas aged in white oak barrels, originally created in limited amounts for private consumption only, to celebrate Don Julio's 45 years in the tequila business. As demand from friends grew, so did production levels, until it was launched on the market in 1996. Brandy-style nose with a hint of agave that opens up as it breathes. Very smooth, light but medium-bodied, with a luscious caramel flavour underlined by agave, and a finish reminiscent of single malt.

TRES MUJERES

Artisan distillery in the lowlands of Jalisco, established in 1996, producing around 2,000 litres daily. Around 95 per cent of production is Reposado, with ex-Bourbon barrels used for ageing.

Blanco, 100 per cent agave, 38 per cent abv.

Reposado, 100 per cent agave, 38 per cent abv. Aged 3 months. A subtle but unmistakable agave nose with a hint of caramel. Deep, smooth agave flavour opens up with a hint of caramel, and a gentle build-up of heat.

Añejo 100 per cent agave, 38 per cent abv. Aged 18 months.

TWO FINGERS

Possibly refering to a double spirit measurement, but with a marketing campaign posing the questions: "Think what you can do with Two Fingers!" and "One night, Two Fingers", the brand obviously has a personality of its own.

Blanco, 40 per cent abv.

Gold Reposado 40 per cent abv. A solid bouquet suggesting dill and fresh herbs, smooth on the palate, with a medium-long finish.

VIUDA DE ROMERO

Distilled in Los Camichines in the highlands of Jalisco, owned by José Cuervo.

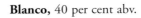

Blanco, 40 per cent abv.

Reposado, 100 per cent agave, 38 per cent abv. Launched in 1997. A full, smooth agave flavour with lovely spicy agave and cinnamon follow-through. Great balance, elegant and rich.

Añejo, 100 per cent agave, 40 per cent abv. Aged 2 years minimum in white oak barrels, resulting in a rich, smooth, velvety character.

TEQUILA LIQUEURS

AGAVERO

32 per cent abv. Launched in 1997 by José Cuervo and produced at Los Camichines distillery in the highlands of Jalisco, using a blend of Reposado and Añejo tequila, together with a herb called damiana (traditionally used in Mexico to flavour liqueurs). Reputed to be an aphrodisiac, damiana grows in Baja California and other regions of north Mexico. The liqueur's rich, earthy tequila bouquet is followed by luscious smoothness with a hint of vanilla and caramel, and a great rounded flavour with a superb Añejo finish.

La Cofradia

The distillery launched a range of liqueurs in 1996, using a base of 100 per cent agave blanco tequila, which is triple distilled for a more subtle agave flavour. The range includes Licor de Café (using coffee from southern Mexico), Licor de Almendra (almond), Licor de Membrillo (quince), and La Pinta (grenadine).

Orendain

Family-owned tequila company using 100 per cent agave Reposado tequila to prepare a range of styles including Crema de membrillo (quince).

Orendain Crema de Almendra. Intense almond aroma with vanilla overtones, through which agave emerges mid-way. Extreme almond, vanilla and caramel flavours include a hint of agave, with a gentle heat build-up, and cloying cherry-brandy style finish.

RIO DE PLATA

Produces Reserva del Señor Licor Natural de Café (coffee), at 26.5 per cent abv, and Oro Viejo licor de almendras (almond) at 30 per cent abv.

MEZCALS

BENEVA

Brand name marketed by the Asociación de Magueyeros de Oaxaca, formed in 1990 to group together various small producers of mezcal from the village of Matatlan, which has a long and distinguished tradition of mezcal production.

Blanco, 38 per cent abv. Bottled immediately after distillation.

Con Gusano ("with the worm"), 38 per cent abv.

Añejo, 38 per cent abv. Aged in oak barrels.

Reserva Tio Pablo Premium mezcal in a glass hand-crafted bottle in the shape of a gusano (worm).

Maya Premium mezcal in a black pyramid-shaped bottle.

ENCANTADO

Blanco, 100 per cent agave, 40 per cent abv. *Encantado* means "enchanted", "bewitched", "placed under magical powers", "delighted" or "in love with". Take your pick. It is also appropriate to say *encantado* on meeting a new friend. The mezcal has an alluring agave aroma with herbaceous hints and smouldering embers, while being rich and full-bodied on the palate, leading to a refreshing, almost citrusy finish.

HACIENDA DE CHIHUAHUA

Reposado, 100 per cent agave, 38 per cent abv. Aged in oak barrels. Very earthy, focused agave nose, ultra-smooth and wonderfully dry on the palate, initially subtle flavours open up with a sandy sensation, and the nature of a well-made artisan drink.

LICORES VERACRUZ

Situated in Cordoba, with a portfolio that includes mezcal, tequila, rum, vodka, liqueurs and aguardiente brands.

Lajita Blanco, 100 per cent agave, 40 per cent abv. Triple distilled, principally from espadin, together with other types of agave, and rested for 40 days in stainless steel tanks to marry the flavours.

Lajita Reposado, 100 per cent agave, 40 per cent abv. Aged in 180 litre white oak barrels. Initially leathery and vegetal before opening up into an aromatic coffee, chocolate bouquet. Subtle on the palate, lightly smoky, vegetal, with a light café au lait chocolatiness before the agave flavour comes through.

Divino. Triple distilled, launched in 1998 by Licores Veracruz, produced using a blend of espadin, criollo and cenizo maguey for an intense agave character.

El Tigre Aguardiente de Cana, 38 per cent abv. Although classified as aguardiente, this is a blend of 15 per cent mezcal and 85 per cent sugar cane spirit, with a slightly sweet, subtle mezcal flavour.

MONTE ALBAN

40 per cent abv. Contains a worm in every bottle. The aroma combines agave with a sprinkling of pepper and fresh smokiness. Agave flavours are laced with a charcoal smokiness and hints of dark chocolate, before a complex follow-through combining charcoal and honey.

PRODUCTOS AGROINDUSTRIALES DE OAXACA

Owned by the Chagoya family, which has produced mezcal in Oaxaca for four generations.

Donaji. Available in various styles including blanco, with the worm, with chilli and aged de luxe (2 years). The company also produces a coffee liqueur – Huatulco Licor de Café.

SAN LUIS DEL RIO

Blanco, 100 per cent agave, 47.8 per cent abv. Leathery, spirited, nail varnish nose. On the palate spicy, peppery, earthy, smoky, barbecued vegetal and agave flavours meld with a hint of chocolate. Robust finish.

TONAYAN

Joven, 100 per cent agave, 40 per cent abv. Agave comes through with caramel and peppery notes, quite smooth though also full-bodied and pungent.

ULTRAMARINE

43 per cent abv, 100 per cent agave. Aged 6 years. Very smoky, charcoal hints on the nose with smoky, luscious caramel and vanilla, and a molten burn, with a chargrilled barbecue flavour coming through.

CHAPTER FOUR

SERVING TEQUILA

SHORT DRINKS

While chilling spirits and serving on the rocks is becoming ever more popular, the effect of this is to heighten the predominant characteristics of the tequila, at the expense of the interesting nuances. Tequila is generally served at room temperature, allowing the aromas and flavours of the more complex styles (and there are plenty of them) to blossom, although chilling is effective when serving Blanco and Reposado. "Shooting", the current term for drinking down in one, may have a certain theatricality to recommend it, but this is obviously not the best way to enjoy tequila's characteristics. It all depends on your priorities – enjoying the flavour or the effect of the alcohol. Blanco and Reposado are typically served in a 50 ml shot glass called a

caballito ("little horse"). Añejo is usually served in a small brandy "snifter". (A large-sized brandy glass is not a good idea, as the large surface area dissipates the aromas too quickly.)

In Mexico the toast with the first shot of tequila is *salud* ("good health"), the second is *dinero* ("wealth"), the third *amor* ("love"), and the fourth *tiempo para disfrutarlos* ("time to enjoy them") – in which case, who wouldn't want at least four shots?

Above
A Mexican bar at the turn of the century, where little else but tequila would have been served.

149

An archetypal, though now clichéd, way to drink tequila is to lick a pinch of salt from between the thumb and forefinger, shoot the tequila, then suck a slice of *limones* (Mexican lemons). In the gringo world it's more often lemon or lime, but this is a poor substitute for limones, which has a wonderfully deep lemon flavour, together with vibrant citrus and grapefruit overtones. The combination of limones and salt is a favourite Mexican accompaniment to various alcoholic drinks, including beer and the Margarita cocktail. The original reason for the salt and limones ritual was entirely practical: tequila was, historically, a robust, if not crude, spirit and the combination of salt and limones provided a full-flavoured distraction. You might wonder why the Mexicans didn't just order something else, but it was the national drink.

Below

Sangrita – the tomato mixer unique to Mexican culture.

Another Mexican tradition prompted by what was originally more robust tequila, is to alternate sips of tequila and sangrita, a highly seasoned tomato juice that is also served in a shot glass. There is no definitive sangrita recipe, though it always includes lemon and orange juice, together with a host of other ingredients such as honey, roasted or fresh chillies, Worcestershire sauce, Tabasco, Maggi, onions and salt. Sangrita is also commercially produced, with some tequila distillers in on the act. Sauza Sangrita is one example, while José Cuervo owns the Viuda de Romero brand that is marketed only in Mexico.

Sangrita plays a key role in "the flag", a popular drinking routine that recreates the colours of the Mexican flag by lining up a glass of tequila, flanked on either side by a glass of sangrita and a glass of lime juice.

Curados (flavoured tequilas) are also popular in Mexico, and are produced by adding favourites such as almond, quince or cinnamon syrup to Blanco or Reposado tequila. Similarly, specialist bars around the world have taken to flavouring Blanco tequila on a DIY basis, introducing a much wider range of ingredients, such as vanilla pods, cinnamon, chilli peppers and even hibiscus tea.

Mexican beer provides another popular tequila "chaser". Sol (meaning "sun") thrives on a clean, crisp, deeply refreshing flavour, and has become something of a fashion icon – although it has actually been brewed for over 100 years. Bohemia is a rich, full-flavoured lager brewed using European hops, while Tecate is a leading brand on the Mexican market. The choice of Dos Equis beers is either Amber, a dark brown malty beer, or Special, a golden style of lager.

Above
Beer is often drunk as a thirst quenching chaser in conjunction with tequila.

LONG DRINKS

Tequila's distinctive agave character means it can be enjoyed with a wide range of mixers without losing its identity. Blanco and Reposado (but not Añejo) are suitable for mixing, with popular combinations being carbonated grapefruit drink, orange juice, apple juice, lemonade, soda water and bitter lemon. However, the most fashionable mixer in Mexico is cola, with Blanco tequila and cola over ice, plus a squeeze of lime juice, known as the Caballa Negro ("black horse"). This is actually a variation of the Cuba Libre rum cocktail, apparently invented in 1893 by a Cuban army lieutenant to celebrate the liberation of Havana. It was also a great way of incorporating what was then the most recent carbonated drink.

While *cazuela* refers to a flat terracotta dish, it is also a way of serving tequila. Carbonated grapefruit drink, grapefruit juice, orange juice, lime juice and ice cubes are combined in such a dish, followed by a shot of Blanco or Reposado tequila, and drunk through a straw. Despite the level of citrus juices in this combination, the agave flavour is actually boosted rather than overwhelmed, and it provides a very refreshing drink.

Opposite
For most Mexicans cola is still the classic tequila mixer.

To prepare a Fresca (also referred to as a Paloma, meaning "dove"), salt is placed in a long glass, and the juice of a limones, lemon or lime wedge is squeezed over it, followed by a measure of Reposado tequila. This is topped up with carbonated

grapefruit drink (a leading brand in Mexico is Squirt, a name that doesn't have the same associations as it does in English). A variation is to substitute cinnamon for the salt, while a simplified but popular version of the Fresca omits the grapefruit drink. The Fresca is reminiscent of the classic Salty Dog, which combines vodka with grapefruit juice, served in a salt-rimmed glass.

The evocatively named Vampiro ("vampire") is a combination of Blanco or Reposado tequila and carbonated grapefruit drink, topped up with sangrita and served on the rocks. Sangrita also plays a key role in Tequila Macho, which comprises Blanco tequila, lime juice and sangrita, with the "macho" element being the addition of a green chilli to be sucked on finishing the drink (beware, as chillies can irritate the skin).

Blanco tequila teams up with another Mexican speciality, Kahlua (a blend of cane spirit and Mexican coffee beans) to produce La Cucaracha ("the cockroach"). This is ignited and drunk from the bottom of the glass using a straw – down in one to prevent the straw from burning (obviously, novices should take care).

Tequila's close relationship with Mexican beer has also resulted in the Submarine, a popular routine throughout Mexico. A shot glass full of Blanco or Reposado tequila is carefully placed inside an upside-down highball glass, so that the base of the highball glass covers and "seals" the top of the shot glass. The shot glass is held in

place while the highball glass is carefully inverted, resulting in the highball glass being the right way up, with an upside-down shot glass resting on the base. Mexican beer is poured into the highball glass, and as sips of beer are taken from the highball glass, the shot glass moves slightly and releases small amounts of tequila. The last few sips of beer require care – to avoid a collision between teeth and shot glass.

A classic approach that has now become rather passé is "slamming", which is referred to as *coscorron* in Jalisco and *moppets* throughout the rest of Mexico. A glass of Blanco tequila topped up with either lemonade or sparkling wine (or even, extravagantly, champagne), is covered using a napkin or simply your hand. This is swirled around before the glass is slammed down on to the bar counter or table top, which sends the contents foaming up the glass, ready to be downed in one. The Mexican tradition is to have a countdown, chanting "un, dos, tres, voom'" as the glass is brought down and the contents knocked back. Some bars, even in Mexico, dispatch tequila girls, who are armed with everything you need for a slamming session at the comfort of your own table. Wearing a customised Mexican bandit's belt, glasses are stored where originally there were bullets, while the tequila girls draw bottles of tequila and sparkling wine or lemonade from their holsters.

TEQUILA COCKTAILS

Cocktails are back in fashion, with the kitsch umbrella and sparklers style of the 1980s replaced by more sophisticated presentations and flavours. Agave's versatile, "user-friendly" characteristics ensure a wide repertoire for blanco and Reposado within established tequila cocktails. Tequila is also making guest appearances in numerous cocktails that have traditionally been the preserve of other spirits.

Brave Bull is an all-Mexican partnership of blanco tequila and Kahlua, stirred over ice and served straight up in a Martini glass.

A French speciality gives the Diabolo a certain *je ne sais quoi*, with anise joining Blanco or Reposado tequila, lime juice, and a dash of caster sugar, which is topped up with either ginger ale or ginger beer.

Silk Stockings is a traditional tequila cocktail now enjoying a fresh wave of popularity. Blanco tequila combines with grenadine, crème de cacao and double cream before being blended with crushed ice.

Long Island Iced Tea, which was particularly popular during the 1980s, comprises blanco tequila, four other white spirits – rum, gin, vodka and Cointreau – and lime juice and cola.

Above
A bull provides an evocative image for a tequila label as well as a spirited cocktail – the Brave Bull.

Another version of this cocktail, Mexican Iced Tea, combines tequila with other Hispanic spirits – pisco (South American grape brandy), cachaca (Brazilian sugar cane spirit) and Havana Club (Cuban rum). The witticism of this cocktail is its resemblance to a glass of iced tea rather than an alcoholic drink. This "design brief" is characteristic of numerous cocktails popular during prohibition in the USA (1919—33).

The Tequila Sunrise, thought to have been created in Mexico during the 1920s, was a prime contender during Prohibition, with a flavour that is dominated by orange juice. (This may sound more attractive than it actually was, since orange juice was generally canned at the time and its flavour so poor that adding sugar was often a necessity.) Achieving the "sunrise" effect for which this cocktail is renowned is simple enough: after pouring tequila and orange juice over ice in a tall glass and stirring well, grenadine is added slowly and settles at the bottom of the glass, creating the sunrise. A professional tip is to place two straws in the glass once the tequila and orange juice have been added, and to pour the grenadine along the junction of the straws. The grenadine will obediently assume its position at the bottom of the glass, without any tell-tale signs on the surface. Grenadine, a non-alcoholic syrup produced from pomegranate juice, is widely used in other cocktails. For a sweeter-tasting Tequila Sunrise, orange juice can be replaced by pineapple juice (the "thin" pineapple juice poured from the top of an unshaken carton is best). Another variation on this theme is the Pink Cadillac, in which Grand Marnier replaces the orange juice. This is an effective substitution that combines flavour with alcoholic strength, as Grand Marnier is produced from the distilled essence of wild tropical oranges blended with Cognac.

The most celebrated tequila cocktail, and always the leader of the cocktail set, is the Margarita, a superlative combination of blanco or Reposado tequila, triple sec (a generic term for orange-flavoured liqueurs) and lime juice, drunk from a glass with a salt-dipped rim.

Such a great cocktail requires a legendary origin, though there are in fact several contenders all claiming to have invented the Margarita. It may date from 1936, when Danny Negrete, the manager of the Crespo Hotel in Puebla, created a drink for his girlfriend. His cue was her passion for the flavour of salt, which meant that she even seasoned her drinks. Then again, it may have happened in Rosarito Beach, Tijuana, in 1938. The inspiration this time was a showgirl, Marjorie King, and the venue a bar called Rancho La Gloria. Marjorie loved to drink but was allergic to all spirits except tequila. The understanding bar owner, Danny Herrera, kept inventing new and exciting ways to serve tequila so that Marjorie didn't get bored. Happily he hit upon the now classic

HER MEXICAN LOVER
by
JEREMY SMITH

9ᴰ.

Thrills and Adventure under Hot Mexican Sun

Right
The Stateside love-affair with Mexican culture has been the biggest single contribution to the rise in tequila's international reputation.

combination and christened it Margarita, the Spanish for Marjorie.

Francisco Pancho Morales also staked his claim. In 1942, at a bar in Cuidad Juarez, a female customer asked him for a "Magnolia", a drink he had vaguely heard of but could only remember that it contained Cointreau. However, rather than admitting this, he improvised and came up with a combination of tequila, Cointreau and lime juice. After all, in case of any complaints, he could always have used the barman's classic stand-by: "Well, that's how we make it here."

So far the common factor is barmen inspired by women, but another possibility is that the Margarita was actually created by an inspired woman – Margarita Sames, the glamorous American socialite of the 1940s. Renowned for giving stylish parties in her Acapulco hacienda, she was thought to have devised this cocktail at a party in 1948. Wanting to impress her illustrious friends, including Nicky Hilton of the hotel family, she combined tequila with Cointreau and lime juice. It was sheer genius.

Yet another possibility is that the Margarita may not even have been created in Mexico. In 1950 a liquor distributor in Los Angeles was delighted but nevertheless mystified by the amount of José Cuervo tequila being ordered by the legendary Tail o' the Cock Restaurant in Beverley Hills. Deciding to get to the bottom of this, he discovered that a tequila-based cocktail called the Margarita had acquired celebrity status, and was adored by the glitterati. Apparently the bartender at the Tail o' the Cock was also a friend of Danny Herrera, the owner of Rancho La Gloria in Tijuana. Small world.

Right
Unmistakeably
Mexican: the
frozen Margarita
stands out from
the crowd.

Ultimately, the most important thing is that we've got the Margarita and what does it matter where it came from. A more appropriate consideration with the Laid-back Margarita is where it goes. It's assembled by the barman, but there's no shaker or glass involved as the constituents of the cocktail are combined in the customer's mouth. This is facilitated by the customer lying down, open-mouthed, on the bar counter or in a special chair (like a dentist's) – with the ingredients better shaken than stirred.

Although long-established as a classic cocktail,

there is still plenty of scope for tailoring the Margarita to personal preferences. A typical ratio, for instance, is 2 parts tequila, 1 part triple sec and 1 part citrus (lime and/or lemon juice). This can be varied to 3 parts tequila, 1 part triple sec and 2 parts lime/lemon juice to make the Margarita Carlos Herrera. Or 3 parts tequila, $1^1/_2$ parts triple sec and 1 part lime/lemon juice.

Using either Blanco or Reposado tequila provides further variety. Blanco tequila is the traditional choice for Margaritas, and this style certainly has a vivid presence, while Reposado is more subtle and is recommended by some bartenders as providing a finer balance with the other ingredients. Similarly, whether triple sec, Cointreau or Grand Marnier is added influences the end result, as Cointreau and Grand Marnier provide a more intense orange flavour (some bartenders adjust the level of tequila accordingly). The Cadillac Margarita takes this a step further, with a "float" of Grand Marnier added to a classic Margarita mix prepared with triple sec, and served on the rocks.

A professional tip for applying salt to the rim of the glass is to wipe just under the outside of the rim with a lemon wedge. This ensures that the salt sticks to the outside of the glass, and doesn't build up on the rim – from where it can fall into the drink. If it does fall in, the salt doesn't dissolve but provides a highly seasoned final sip.

Any cocktail as enduring as the Margarita is obviously going to evolve and yield variations on the theme. Consequently, the Frozen Margarita and the Fruit Flavoured Margarita, not to mention the Frozen Fruit Margarita, have each proved to be a great step forward.

The wonderfully refreshing Frozen Margarita means blending all the ingredients with crushed ice to produce a sorbet effect, though more liquid than solid. As the flavour of tequila is inhibited by chilling, this is an ideal style of Margarita for a novice.

The simplest way of incorporating fruit flavours within a Margarita is by using either a flavoured tequila or a fruit juice – pomegranate juice, for instance, combined with grenadine and a drop of triple sec is an effective combination. Adding sliced fruit, such as peaches, kiwi fruit or strawberries, and shaking the fruit together with a classic Margarita mix before straining the liquid into a glass also produces good results. Similarly, fruits such as blueberries can be puréed together with a dash of sugar syrup and blue curaçao and a Margarita mix. Alternatively, puréed strawberries, mangoes or peaches can be combined with tequila, a little caster sugar, a dash of water and $1/2$ a chopped lime in a cocktail shaker filled with rock ice (which gives better flavour penetration). After vigorous shaking, the liquid is strained through a conical sieve. Adding a dash of orange bitters to the cocktail mix also helps to balance various fruit flavours.

To prepare a Frozen Fruit Margarita, a small amount of sugar, fruit and the relevant fruit liqueur (to help bring out the fruit flavour) are added to the classic mix, together with crushed ice. Different fruit also has varying affinities with Blanco and Reposado tequila. Peach, for instance, combines well with Reposado.

When serving fruit-flavoured Margaritas, the rim of the glass can be either left plain or dipped in caster sugar. Alternatively, a combination of caster sugar and salt can be used, which adds a savoury note that prevents the cocktail from potentially tasting like a fruit punch. Flavoured Margaritas are usually served in an oversized Martini glass.

MARGARITA PRE-MIXES

In this era of convenience products, it's inevitable that pre-mixes are becoming ever-more popular. José Cuervo and Sauza, for instance, produce not only the tequila to make a Margarita, but also a non-alcoholic Margarita mix with which to combine it.

D.L. Jardine's Texarita Margarita Mix was the result of a tragic love affair. The legendary D.L. Jardine, founder of the D.L. Jardine drinks

Above
Cuervo's ready-made mixer for the now legendary cocktail.

company in the USA, fell in love with Rita del Rio, the most sensational woman to be seen along the Texas-Mexico border. In fact, drawn by her shimmering black hair and alluring blue eyes, men travelled from far and wide to the Café Eldorado in the small town of Los Ebanos where Rita prepared her fabulous Margaritas. Despite this widespread adulation, Rita was a "one-man woman" and that man was D.L. Jardine. During his long absences travelling the Chisholm Trail, Rita sat on her front porch throughout the night, singing love songs and sipping Margaritas, waiting for D.L. to return. One summer night, in his absence, some bandits rode into town and abducted Rita from her porch. D.L. searched the border for months to find her, but never did. All he found was her Margarita recipe, which he subsequently passed on to the next generation of Jardines. It must have been some consolation, because this pre-mix tastes great.

TEQUILA STEPS INTO CLASSIC COCKTAILS

Beyond its own exclusive range, tequila is also diversifying into classic cocktails traditionally the domain of other spirits, and is providing them with a fresh new angle.

As if the name doesn't say it all, the Bloody Maria is a tequila variation of the Bloody Mary, a drink that has already experienced one makeover, having originally been a gin cocktail before vodka supplanted gin in the 1920s. This was a perfectly logical progression, as vodka has a far better affinity than gin with tomato juice and the variable cast of seasonings such as lemon juice, Worcestershire sauce, celery salt, cayenne and horseradish. The Bloody Maria is not simply a case of tequila trying to cash in on vodka's success with the Bloody Mary, as tequila's relationship with sangrita proves the great rapport between the two, particularly when Blanco tequila is being used. Indeed, the Bloody Maria is more a case of extending the relationship between tequila and sangrita by drinking them together rather than separately.

Tequila is also making inroads on the Dry Martini, which enjoys greater mystique and allure, and consequently a more fanatical following, than any other cocktail. The Dry

Martini is another instance of vodka taking over what was originally a gin-based cocktail, though the opportunities for tequila to duplicate vodka's success in this instance are limited. Apart from the awkward amalgam used to describe the Tequila Martini – Tequilini – tequila doesn't have the same affinity with vermouth, though the best results are obtained using thoroughly chilled Blanco. But, as soon as the temperature begins to rise, the combination begins to lose its edge.

The Cosmopolitan is currently riding high in the fashion stakes, being an effective combination of clear or flavoured vodka, with Cointreau, cranberry juice and lime juice. The Tequila Cosmopolitan has, so far, remained in the shadows of the original. The best examples are adaptations of the original recipe, using either Blanco or Reposado combined with Cytrynowka (Polish lemon vodka), orange curaçao, and a dash each of orange bitters, lime cordial and fresh lime juice. You may, of course, say this is not a Cosmopolitan – and I wouldn't argue.

Brandy Sour, which originated in the mid-19th century, has led the way for several variations, notably the Whiskey Sour. Tequila is also having its turn in the Sour category, capitalising on Blanco's natural affinity with lemon juice, while adding sugar is no problem either.

Following the tradition pioneered by Irish coffee (coffee flavoured with Irish whiskey), blanco and Reposado tequila are also established additions to coffee, though this is far from being an institution in Mexico. Nevertheless, it is a great combination of two natural assets, with Mexican coffee renowned for being rich and full-bodied. The Mexican coffee industry, dating from the 1800s, doesn't have the same antiquity as tequila and mezcal, though there is some overlap in the production areas, with Oaxaca, the heartland of mezcal production, also being a source of coffee beans, as are Hidalgo and Veracruz.

FLAVOURING TEQUILA

While commercially flavoured tequilas incorporating coffee, almond and cinnamon are available (but must be marketed as liqueurs), flavouring tequila on a DIY basis is simple. Effective results can be obtained by infusing herbs, spices and other flavourings in blanco tequila. Vanilla pods, coffee beans, pineapple chunks, and lemon or lime wedges, for instance, will take about two weeks in tequila at 40 per cent abv. To convert blanco into a caramel style, sugar syrup can be added to blanco tequila before it begins to set. The proportion of flavourings used, and when the tequila is "ready", are obviously a matter of personal preference, so tastings should be conducted en route.

CHAPTER FIVE

TEQUILA AND FOOD

The food and drink of a country or region inevitably evolve together and, because of tequila's central role in Mexico, it has developed an integral relationship with food. Indeed, Mexican food ranges from the subtle and elegant to the spicy and robust, just like the different styles of tequila, whether served neat or in a cocktail like the Margarita.

A great advantage of serving tequila in true Mexican style is that tequila is always accompanied by botanas – not just any old snacks, but a specific range of hors d'oeuvres. A common denominator of botanas is robust, spicy, salty flavours, which quite effortlessly encourage further rounds of tequila. But there is also a genuine relationship between tequila and the food as the flavours do actually harmonise on the palate.

Opposite
Tequila and Mexican food go together like a cowboy and his horse.

As well as performing a balancing act, tequila promotes the flavours of archetypal botanas such as *cueritos* (boiled pig skin marinaded in vinegar, thyme, pepper and bay leaf), *chicharron* (fried

pork crackling), and *barbacoa* (barbecued lamb). Moreover, tequila helps to cut through the richness of favourites such as panella, a lightly salty, crumbly cow's milk cheese, an effect heightened when the panella is served in a fried tortilla. Fried tortillas, which are almost always corn- rather than flour-based, envelope endless combinations, such as finely chopped chicken with tomato, onion and garlic, which are rolled up inside a tortilla and sliced to provide finger food.

Another great favourite is guacamole – puréed avocado with onions, tomato and various seasonings. The importance of the avocado pear in Mexican cuisine is inevitable, considering that Mexico is the world's largest producer of the fruit. In fact, Mexico's annual production of 700,000 tons represents about a third of the world total. Tortilla with guacamole is perfectly partnered by a smooth, elegant Reposado tequila such as Don Julio, which spices up the avocado flavour before releasing a wave of avocado creaminess.

Cactus salad (chopped cactus with tomato and onion, sprinkled with sea salt) on a fried tortilla also works well with Reposado, which enhances the cactus flavour beautifully after the initial spiciness of the agave.

Gorditas "flattie" tortilla (which resembles an English muffin with a puffy texture) can be served simply with butter and salt. After the first spicy flush of Reposado, the gorditas' rich butteriness comes through loud and clear, together with a hint of salt.

Adding chilli sauce to this type of tortilla also results
in the chilli flavour emerging appetisingly through
the agave effect.

All the flavours of a shrimp, pineapple, onion
and cucumber salad served on a fried tortilla are
heightened by Don Julio Reposado, while the
agave flavours of the tequila benefit by gaining
an even spicier edge. On the other hand,
Reposado tones down the inferno quality of

chillies in *camarones agua chilli* (shrimp with chilli on a fried tortilla), while the agave also provides an extra layer of seasoning.

A wonderfully refreshing botanas dish, and also an effective palate cleanser, is *pico de gallo*, a combination of finely chopped cucumber, *jicama* (a Mexican white root vegetable with a firm, tender texture), pineapple, carrot and orange, seasoned with lime juice, salt and ground chilli.

Opposite

Despite its alcoholic strength tequila, like wine, spans a wide range of characteristics so it can be tailored to suit almost any dish.

MATCHING DISHES

Not surprisingly, outside Mexico there is often a mental block about drinking tequila or mezcal with food, and a spirit that's around 38-40 per cent abv inevitably suggests alcoholic excess. A measure of tequila actually contains the same level of alcohol as a glass of wine, though obviously tequila is not drunk in the same quantities. And when it comes to matching tequila with food, botanas prove that tequila can match a range of different dishes. After all, flavour combinations are what it's all about.

MATCHING WITH MEXICAN FOODS

While botanas play a supporting role to tequila during the aperitif hour, it is more usual for tequila to be tailored to the food during a meal. Not that this will impose any restrictions: like wine, tequila spans a wide range of characteristics: from dry to rich and luscious; from earthy and herbaceous to vegetal and spicy.

A classic Mexican starter is a logical place to begin: fried tortilla soup, prepared from chicken stock, tomatoes and chillies and garnished with fried tortilla pieces, chopped avocado, crumbled cheese and a squeeze of limones. Teamed with Tapatillo Añejo, the soup's rich, robust flavours become spicier and even more "molten".

Shrimp *tostada* (shrimp, chopped red onion and chopped tomato wrapped in a toasted tortilla) is great with José Cuervo Tradicional. This yields an initial wave of agave flavour followed by tomato and herbaceous notes before the shrimp flavours surface. The finish is a mouthful of lingering herbaceousness. Centenario Reposado is also an ultra-smooth partner, promoting a subtle interplay of flavours.

A taco of pork, chopped avocado and red onion wrapped in a corn tortilla is spiced up by José Cuervo Tradicional, which also makes the meat juicier and promotes a spicy aftertaste. The same tequila provides a spicy undertone when accompanying fillet steak with an orange sauce that incorporates blanco tequila.

Similarly, beefsteak Mexicana (strips of fried beef with tomato, chopped onion and green chilli) receives an additional layer of seasoning, and the meat is juicier when taken with Tapatillo Añejo.

A classic example of Nuova Cocina Mexicana (New Wave Mexican Cuisine), is cheese quesadillas with rose petal stuffing and rosewater, accompanied by strawberry sauce. A Margarita prepared with Sauza blanco harmonises all the flavours while softening the pastry wrapper and giving the cheese a lovely molten quality. The cocktail's integral saltiness also adds an extra layer of seasoning that perks up all the flavours.

Another example of this contemporary cooking style is shrimp served with guajillo cream (cream flavoured with a very mild green chilli) and huitlacoche-style rice (flavoured with a highly-desirable black fungus that develops on sweetcorn). This dish combines well with a Margarita using Sauza Reposado, which brings out the meatiness of the shrimps and the creaminess of the guajillo, while the cocktail's saltiness adds an integral layer of seasoning.

Margaritas can not only replace wine at the table but they deal successfully with a range of flavours that would easily overpower wine. While they are increasingly drunk with food in the USA and UK, this is not the practice in Mexico.

The international popularity of the Caesar salad makes it easy to forget that it was actually created in Mexico. This dish wasn't named after a Roman emperor, nor is it connected with Caesar's Palace in Las Vegas (which also has no connection with any emperor). The eponymous creator of the salad (surname Cardini) was an Italian emigrant who ran a restaurant in Tijuana. On the fourth of July in 1924, a party of

Americans checked in for lunch and asked for something totally different with which to celebrate their national holiday. It was a case of going to the kitchen, taking what was to hand and combining these ingredients in a moment of inspiration – or so the story goes. The Americans loved it, extracted the recipe from Señor Cardini and took it back with them to Los Angeles. From there, "the Caesar" cast its spell all over America, and the rest of the salad-eating world followed suit.

Many chefs claim to use Caesar Cardini's original recipe, but as there are so many variations around, deciding on the definitive version is impossible. Nevertheless, the salad comprises cos lettuce dressed with a combination of olive oil, garlic, vinegar, lemon juice, Dijon mustard and Worcestershire sauce, with anchovies, added either in the form of essence to the dressing, or whole in the salad. Similarly, an egg cooked for one minute is either incorporated into the dressing, tossed with the leaves or cracked on top of the salad. Parmesan and a scattering of garlic croûtons is the final touch.

Opposite
Many a visitor has discoverd the spirit of Mexico and taken it home with them whether it's in the form of handicrafts or the country's food and drink.

Caesar salad thrives in the company of tequila, with Herradura Blanco melting the croûtons and the Parmesan, while also spicing up the dressing, and resulting in a follow-through of fresh lettuce flavours. Centinela Añejo and Caesar salad initially combine to create a new range of flavours, before the salad flavours emerge underpinned by agave seasoning.

178

MATCHING WITH
INTERNATIONAL CUISINES

Tequila combines so well with Mexican dishes that its rapport with other cuisines is often overlooked. But, however diverse the menu, the same principles apply. This means that cream and cheese, for example, benefit from the tequila effect that cuts through the richness to create a molten sensation. Similarly, pastry is softened and

179

meat becomes much juicier, while tequila's herbaceous and spicy characteristics provide an additional layer of seasoning. Blanco and Reposado are generally the most effective partners for a wide range of dishes, although Añejo's vanilla and caramel notes can also provide a good match.

Considering the influential role the Spanish played in the development of tequila, not to mention other cultural aspects of Mexico, an obvious starting point is to combine tequila and mezcal with Spanish tapas.

The saltiness and acidity of fresh anchovies are initially subdued by El Tesoro Silver tequila and Lajita Reposado mezcal, then the anchovy flavours resurface and combine harmoniously with the agave, before they gently fade out together. Similarly, the richness of Sauza Tres Generaciones at first overwhelms the anchovies, before striking a balance and allowing the anchovy flavours to come forth on equal terms.

Iberico ham benefits enormously from El Tesoro Reposado and Sauza Tres Generaciones. Not only do the flavours complement each other, but the tequila cuts through the fattiness of the ham and even acts as a palate cleanser.

Chorizo is initially subdued by El Tesoro Silver before the flavours combine into a great double act, with the chorizo becoming spicier and juicier. Monte Alban mezcal also balances the spiciness of chorizo, making the meat wonderfully tender and juicy, while the chorizo smoothes the agave flavours.

The spiciness of potatoes with chillies, paprika and peppers is greatly enhanced by Sauza Conmemorativo, while Sauza Blanco adds a milder degree of spice, allowing the food flavours to emerge more readily.

The caramelised, lightly smoky flavours of chargrilled vegetables are emphasised by Lajita Reposado mezcal, which particularly highlights onions and aubergine.

Roasted pepper salad is boosted by El Tesoro silver, which really brings out the juicy sweetness of the peppers. Similarly, El Tesoro Reposado smoothes the pepper flavours beautifully, with a lingering follow-through of caramelised sweetness. The benefit of Sauza Conmemorativo is the melding of the peppers and agave flavours, which are laced with a caramelised sweetness.

Tuna and salmon carpaccio with red onions, chilli and olive oil works well with El Tesoro

Opposite
El Tesoro connoisseur range – each distinct type and brand of tequila can bring something new to the right dish.

silver, making the dish incredibly smooth while also yielding a lovely, spicy follow-through.

Beyond Hispanic dishes, there is a world of gastronomic opportunities – some of which come from unexpected sources. Herrings, for instance, are a staple of northern and eastern European cuisines, and are also a feature of modern British cooking – but provenance is irrelevant when it comes to flavour combinations.

Herring and beetroot salad with sour cream benefits from Tres Magueyes Blanco tequila, which reduces the saltiness of the herrings, lightens the cream and enrichens the subtle beetroot flavour. If you prefer the flavours to be fortissimo, then Tres Magueyes Reposado obliges, emphasising the herring and onion with an underlying spiciness. Similarly, Centenario Reposado provides a base of agave flavour that highlights the ingredients.

With another seafood combination – clams with seaweed and spring onion – Tres Magueyes blanco emphasises the clams' "sea-salt" quality and the freshness of the spring onion before a lovely agave flavour laced with clams provides a lingering follow–through.

Why bother having white wine with grilled halibut accompanied by cabbage, fennel and mustard, when tequila does the job in a more interesting way? Admittedly, tequila briefly overwhelms the dish, but the flavours do co-operate subsequently. Tres Magueyes Blanco adds a warm herbaceous and juicy quality to the fish, while Tres Magueyes Reposado enlivens the fish with "agave seasoning".

Grilled prime rib of beef requires a moment to emerge through Tres Magueyes Blanco, which then promotes the beef's lightly "caramelised" flavours and makes the texture even more tender. Centenario Reposado also makes the meat juicier, and introduces a subtle layer of seasoning mid-way, while Don Julio Añejo achieves the same rapport, with a wonderfully meaty follow-through.

Tequila can continue quite happily throughout a meal. Pear and almond tart with vanilla ice cream is subtly emphasised by Tres Magueyes Blanco, which evokes the richness of the apples and nuttiness of the almonds. Meanwhile, the caramel notes in Reposado harmonise all the flavours, melt the pastry, and provide an effective counterpoint to the ice cream.

Rhubarb syllabub sandwiched between light shortbread sprinkled with icing or caster sugar is a feast of rich flavours that Tres Magueyes blanco tackles head on – melting the shortbread beautifully, while creamy rhubarb flavours emerge mid-way, heightened by the underlying agave. Reposado also brings out the depth of flavours, while Don Julio Añejo highlights the wonderful sweetness of the rhubarb and cream, as well as the sugar on the shortbread, in a rich, molten mouthful.

Chocolate is a renowned problem area for many

drinks as cocoa coats the tongue, but tequila can help here. Indeed, white and dark chocolate terrine is marvellous with Sauza Tres Generaciones. The agave flavour really perks up the chocolate, and the chocolate smoothes the agave flavour, while both the chocolate and tequila still retain their independence on the palate.

TEQUILA IN COOKING

Just as tequila can be an ideal accompaniment to food, it can be an effective flavouring in various sweet or savoury dishes. Tequila's alcoholic content and "body" also ensure that it is a valuable culinary asset.

The general principle of cooking with wines or spirits is to boil off all the alcohol. However, retaining some alcohol (by either adding it towards the end of cooking or by topping up with more alcohol at the last minute) means it contributes a significant amount of flavour and body. Using tequila as a cooking ingredient does not mean you can get away with a poor-quality brand. Cooking eliminates only the alcohol content; it does not improve the flavour of the tequila, so you only get back what you put in.

As all alcoholic drinks can be used as flavourings in cooking, many countries have developed their own traditions of cooking with alcohol. This means that there are many international roles for tequila to step into. Rice wine, for instance, stipulated in numerous Asian dishes, can be replaced with tequila. The same applies to rum in Caribbean and brandy in French cuisines, particularly for a flambé.

Traditional Mexican recipes certainly make the most of tequila. Black bean soup is an example, based on a purée of black beans, garlic and *episote* (an earthy-flavoured Mexican herb), cooked in chicken stock with Blanco tequila. This style of tequila can also be used to finish a chilled gazpacho, utilising the long-established rapport between tequila and the tomato drink sangrita.

Another traditional Mexican soup, served on Thursdays, is *pozole* ("corn grain"). A hearty soup, it contains pork and chicken cooked in chicken stock, and is thickened with corn grains prior to being fortified by mezcal. The soup is also served with a glass of mezcal on the side, not to mention a range of botanas such as chicken tacos and radish slices. Regional variations of the dish include the addition of ground pumpkin seeds (turning the soup green) in Acapulco and the state of Guereno, while adding red chillies and tomatoes is typical in the north of Mexico. Not surprisingly, after such a heavy meal (with lunch usually served between 3 and 4 pm), a return to the office is not guaranteed, nor is it necessarily desirable.

A ceviche, the term for raw fish marinated in citrus juices, might include Mexican favourites like red snapper and shark, while a seafood ceviche typically features octopus, oysters, shrimps and a selection of fish. The marinade can combine lime or lemon juice with other ingredients such as tomato, onion, garlic, chilli sauce and Blanco tequila. Any marinade remaining after cooking can accompany the fish and seafood as a sauce. A marinade can also be adapted into a relish, with a "tequila relish" an ideal accompaniment to seafood favourites such as crab cakes.

As alcohol tenderises meat, a tequila-based marinade is best prepared using blanco, which offers the highest level of agave flavour. Additional ingredients also influence the end result, with papaya and tequila, for instance, being an ideal tropical-style marinade for beef. The marinade also provides the basis for a cooking liquor and afterwards a sauce, needing only to be reduced and flavoured with the likes of herbs, spices, stock and cream.

Deglazing is another method of creating an instant sauce: add tequila to the pan after sautéeing or roasting meat, raise the heat and blend the tequila with the cooking juices, while scraping any remnants from the surface of the pan. Once the alcohol has boiled off (or not, as you prefer), the finishing touches can be added. *Salsa Borracho*, meaning "drunk sauce", is a Mexican favourite prepared using either mezcal or pulque. Plum tomatoes, green chillies, garlic and onions are seared on a high heat to caramelise their surfaces before being puréed with mezcal or pulque. This sauce is ideal with full-flavoured meat like barbecued beef or goat.

Gusano from agave has always been considered a gourmet item, and is even served in such a chic location as the restaurant at the Four Seasons Hotel in Mexico City. Sautéed in a little oil with onions, garlic and chilli, it is served in a tortilla accompanied by guacamole, green sauce (prepared from green tomatoes), coriander and chopped onions.

As well as being a traditional cooking accessory, tequila is also an integral element of Nuova Cocina Mexicana, in which classic dishes are brought up to date. Shrimps, for instance, are cooked with garlic and chillies before being flamed with blanco tequila. A more elaborate version sees giant shrimps stuffed with pieces of cheese inserted into a pocket created by slicing the shrimps lengthways. The stuffed shrimps are marinaded in blanco tequila before being flamed in a pan containing olive oil and garlic.

A flambé not only looks spectacular, but the flames help to brown the food as well as caramelising any sugar content. Tequila should be pre-heated to below boiling point (cold tequila could be absorbed by the food, which would defeat the object), and lit before being poured over the dish. The flames simply extinguish themselves once the alcohol has expired. Chicken breasts in a tequila-flavoured cream sauce can be prepared using this technique, the meat being fried in butter with garlic and onion, flamed in tequila, then simmered in cream before being served garnished with fresh herbs.

Tequila is also on call to help with the simplest of desserts. Simply sprinkle a rich Reposado over ready-prepared fruit, or allow a more leisurely maceration. Or, when flambéing a dessert such as crêpes suzette, why not use a Reposado tequila, particularly as the residual flavour is mellower than brandy?

As tequila provides a concentrated flavour within a small amount of liquid, it makes an ideal flavouring for ice cream and sorbets. It also improves the texture since alcohol has a lower freezing point than water, which helps prevent the formation of sugar crystals and achieves a smoother result. (Adding whisked egg white is a traditional means of improving texture, but the flavour is diminished in the process.) However, too much tequila is not good either, as the alcohol content will inhibit the freezing process. Utilising tequila's affinity with sangrita, a tomato or sangrita sorbet would act equally well as a savoury dessert or a palate cleanser. Alternatively, if you don't actually use tequila within the sorbet or ice-cream, you can pour Blanco tequila over lemon ice cream, or Reposado over vanilla or chocolate ice cream, to provide an instant sauce.

Syllabub is a classic English dessert dating from the reign of Elizabeth I, then a combination of double cream and white wine, beaten to create a thicker texture. Subsequently, whisky, brandy and rum have all been used instead of wine, which means that tequila is also a prime contender, particularly when the syllabub is flavoured with exotic fruits such as guava. For a lighter style of syllabub with a softer texture, combine double cream with natural yoghurt.

A classic Mexican dessert is sliced pineapple poached in sugar syrup, to which Blanco tequila is added. Extra blanco can also be poured on the pineapple and flamed. Equally traditional is a tequila "custard pie", a set custard prepared from tequila, white wine, eggs and sugar, with Reposado's vanilla and caramel flavours being most complimentary.

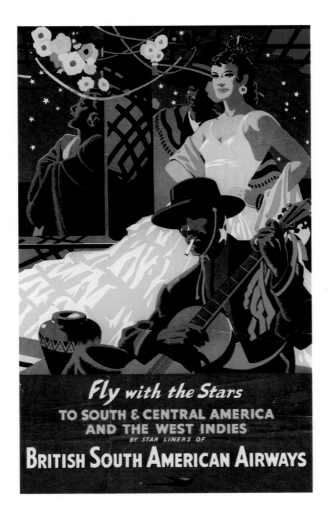

RECIPES

BLACK BEAN SOUP

Heat the oil in a large saucepan, add the bacon and sauté until all the fat is rendered. Add the onion, garlic, celery and chilli and cook until tender. Add the beans and stock, bring to the boil and boil hard for 10 minutes, then lower the heat and simmer for about 2 hours until the beans are tender. Purée the mixture, strain back into the saucepan and reheat. Season to taste and adjust the consistency with extra chicken stock, if necessary. Serve in bowls garnished with coriander and the tequila cream, accompanied by the tortilla strips.

Serves 4

60 ml/4 tbsp olive oil
30 g/1 oz diced bacon
60 g/2½ oz onion, finely diced
10 g/½ oz minced garlic
30 g/1 oz minced celery
1 piece serrano chilli
500 g/1lb 2 oz black beans
2.5 litres/4½ pts boiling chicken stock
Salt and pepper
Coriander leaves
Tequila cream, made from 60 g/2½ oz soured cream beaten with 30 ml/2 tbsp blanco tequila, refrigerated
60 g/2½ oz corn tortillas, cut into thin strips

TEQUILA SHRIMP WITH GARLIC CHIPS AND GUAJILLO CHILLI

2 elephant garlic cloves (or largest available size), thinly sliced
15 ml/1 tbsp olive oil
24 jumbo shrimps, peeled, deveined and refrigerated
30 g/1 oz guajillo chilli, cut into 1.5 ml/½ in thick slices
30 ml/2 tbsp blanco tequila
120 g/4½ oz butter
Juice of 1 lemon
60 g/2½ oz tomato, finely diced
50 g/2 oz snipped chives

Fry the garlic in a little of the oil until golden brown, remove from pan and reserve. Sauté the shrimps in the same oil. Add the chilli and when crisp add the tequila and flame the pan. Remove and reserve the shrimps and chilli. Add the butter and swirl round the pan over a low flame until the sauce thickens. Return the shrimps and chilli to the pan and reheat, adding the lemon juice. Divide shrimps between four plates and serve each accompanied by some of the reserved garlic chips, diced tomato and chives.

Serves 4

CEVICHE

Combine the marinade ingredients. Arrange the fish and seafood in a shallow non-metallic dish, cover and chill for 4-6 hours. Serve chilled garnished with a wedge of lime to squeeze over.

Serves 4 as a starter

For the marinade:

15 ml/1 tbsp lime juice

15 ml/1 tbsp grated lime zest

120 ml/4 fl oz/½ cup lemon juice

15 ml/1 tbsp red chillies puréed with a dash of olive oil

½ bunch coriander, chopped

A pinch of salt

200 ml/7 fl oz coconut milk (optional)

50 ml/2 fl oz 100 per cent agave reposado tequila

For the fish:

225 g/8 oz raw fresh salmon, finely diced

100 g/4 oz raw fresh scallops

100 g/4 oz sliced raw fresh tiger prawn

4 rock oysters

Lime wedges

For the relish:

2 ripe papayas, peeled and cut into 1.5 cm/ ½ in dice

1 tomato, peeled, cored, seeded and diced

½ small red onion, cut into 1.5 ml/¼ in dice

1 garlic clove, finely chopped

2 small chillies, seeded and finely chopped

15 ml/ 1 tbsp finely chopped fresh coriander

2.5 ml/½ tsp chilli powder

Juice of 1 lemon

Salt

50 ml/2 fl oz tequila

For the crab cakes:

1 egg, beaten

15 ml/1 tbsp mayonnaise

2.5 ml/½ tsp paprika

1.5 l/½ tsp ground black pepper

1.5 ml/¼ tsp curry powder

1.5 ml/¼ tsp mustard powder

1.5 ml/¼ tsp cayenne pepper

15 ml/1 tbsp Worcestershire sauce

15 ml/1 tbsp lemon juice

3 drops Tabasco sauce

500 g/1lb 2 oz fresh white crab meat

20 ml/1½ tbsp dry breadcrumbs

Vegetable oil, for shallow frying

SPICY CRAB CAKES ON PAPAYA WITH TEQUILA RELISH

Combine all the relish ingredients in a bowl, and allow to stand for at least 10 minutes. To prepare the crab cakes combine the egg, mayonnaise and seasonings. Add the crab meat and enough of the breadcrumbs to absorb any excess moisture. Stir the ingredients to blend them, but do not over-mix. The mixture should be just firm enough to hold together. Adjust the seasoning. Form the mixture into 12 patties and place on greaseproof paper and chill in the fridge for 20 minutes to dry slightly. Pour the oil into a frying pan to a depth of 2.5 cm/1in. Over a high heat, carefully add the crab cakes and fry for about 3 minutes on each side until golden brown. Drain on paper towel and serve immediately on the relish.

Serves 4

LOBSTER AND TEQUILA CEVICHE

Combine the marinade ingredients and purée. Place in a small bowl, cover with clingfilm and reserve. For the ceviche, combine all the ingredients, cover with clingfilm and refrigerate. To serve, arrange some of the ceviche in the centre of the plate, spoon the marinade over and around, and garnish with coriander.

Serves 4

For the marinade:

Juice of 1 orange

Juice of 2 limes

15 ml/1 tbsp Dijon mustard

15 ml/1 tbsp grated horseradish

¼ small white onion, diced

30 ml/2 tbsp lobster or fish stock

50 ml/2 fl oz tequila

For the ceviche:

2 lobsters, about 750 g/ 1lb 8 oz each, boiled, shelled, diced and chilled

1 medium tomato, peeled, seeded and diced

½ small red onion, peeled and thinly sliced

8 coriander sprigs, chopped

2 spring onions, trimmed and shredded

½ small bunch chives, chopped

SALSA BORRACHA
(DRUNKEN SAUCE)

500 g/1lb 2 oz tomatoes,
  skinned, seeded and chopped
100 g/3½ oz onion, finely
  chopped
50 g/2 oz green chilli, finely
  chopped
1 bunch coriander, chopped
25 g/1 oz ancho chilli,
  chopped
50 ml/2 fl oz 100 per cent
  agave reposado tequila
Lime juice

Combine all the ingredients and leave for at least 30 minutes to allow the flavours to develop. Serve with grilled fish or chicken.

BLACK CHERRY SAUCE

Sweat the shallots, chilli, ginger and garlic until soft but not browned. Add the cherries, including the juice from the can, and the tequila. Allow the sauce to reduce for 1-2 minutes, then serve with lamb fillet or grilled duck breast.

100 g/3½ oz shallots, chopped
25 g/1 oz red chilli, chopped
50 g/2 oz fresh root ginger,
* finely chopped*
50 g/2 oz garlic, crushed
250 g/9 oz canned black
* cherries*
60-75 ml/4-5 tbsp 100 per
* cent agave reposado tequila*

GUAVA LIME AND TEQUILA SYLLABUB

300 ml/½ pt double cream
60 g/2½ oz caster sugar
Juice of 1½ limes
2 guavas, peeled, liquidised
   and sieved
60 ml/4 tbsp tequila

Whip the cream with the sugar until fairly stiff. Slowly add the lime juice while whipping continuously, then incorporate the guava purée and tequila. Serve the syllabub in tall glasses or brandy snaps, garnished with a selection of sliced tropical fruits.

Serves 4

TEQUILA LIME SORBET

Bring the water to the boil and stir in the sugar until completely dissolved. Add the lime juice and zest, then stir in the tequila. Freeze the mixture, stirring thoroughly every 30 minutes to break up the crystals, until frozen. Serve with an extra splash of Añejo tequila.

600 ml/1 pt water
350 g/12 oz caster sugar
Juice and finely grated zest of 8 limes
75 ml/5 tbsp 100 per cent agave reposado tequila Añejo

Serves 4

TEQUILA GAZETTEER
SELECTED TEQUILA VENUES

MEXICO
La Destileria, Av Mexico 2016 esq Nelson, Guadalajara
El Abajeno, Av Juarez, San Pedro Tlaquepaque, Guadalajara
El Presidente Hotel, Av Lopez Mateos Sur y Moctezuma Cd. del Sol, Guadalajara
La Destileria, Homero y Vazquez de Mella, Pabellon Polanco, Mexico City
Four Seasons Hotel, Paseo de la Reforma 500, Mexico City
The Ritz-Carlton, Retorno Del Rey 36, Zon Hotelera, Cancun

FRANCE
Café Pacifico, 50 Boulevard Montparnasse, Paris
La Perla, 26 Rue François Miron, Paris

NETHERLANDS
Café Pacifico, 31 Warmoesstraat 31, Amsterdam

UNITED KINGDOM
Navajo Joe, 34 King Street, London WC2
Cactus Blue, 86 Fulham Road, London SW3
Café Pacifico, 5 Langley Street, London WC2
La Perla, 28 Maiden Lane, London WC2

UNITED STATES
Fifty Seven Fifty Seven Bar, Four Seasons Hotel, 57 East 57th Street, New York
Left at Albuquerque, 2140 Union Street, San Francisco
Salpicon, 1252 North Wells, Chicago

INDEX

ACKNOWLEDGEMENTS

The writing of this book was greatly helped by Ramon Gonzalez Figueroa of the Tequila Regulatory Council in Guadalajara; Patricia Moreno of Bancomext in London, and the Bancomext staff in Guadalajara; Ryder Butler of Maxwell's Restaurant Group; Don Julio Gonzalez of Tres Magueyes; Su-Lin Ong; Sam Chadha and José Cuervo International; Cliff Hatch from Sauza; Mezcal Monte Alban; Licores Veracruz; the Anthropology Museum in Mexico City; Pete Murray and Jeannie Estes of Café Pacifico; Legends restaurant; Lupita Rios and the Presidente Inter-Continental Hotel in Guadalajara; Melanie Baker of Inter-Continental Hotels in London; Sue Lowry of Columbus Communications; the Four Seasons Hotel in Mexico City; Jasper Eyears; Cairbry Hill and Albero & Grana restaurant; La Destileria restaurant in Mexico City; Dale Sklar of Wine & Spirit International; Tequila La Gonzalena; Porfidio; Sotol de Chihuahua, Vinomex; Dethleffsen International.

For the recipes thanks to Paul Gayler of the Lanesborough Hotel and Richard Ellis of Navajo Joe in London, and Glen Eastmann of the Four Seasons Hotel in Mexico City.

I would like to thank the following companies for allowing me to visit their distilleries, and answering endless questions: José Cuervo, Sauza, Centinela, Tequila Tapiato, Tequilas del Señor, La Arandina, Seagram, Herradura, Cofradia, Tres Magueyes, Tres Mujeres and Cazadores.

PICTURE CREDITS

Encantado 95, 144; La Gonzaleña 32; Herradura 47, 49, 64, 67, 73, 76, 78, 85, 122; José Cuervo International 23, 40, 50, 62, 89, 119, 162, 166, 173; Mary Evans/Explorer 11; Sauza International 14, 26, 43, 45, 57, 59, 70, 131, 132, 174, 180; The Vintage Magazine Co. 7, 18, 29, 55, 91, 106, 153, 155, 160, 171, 179, 198. Agavero 142; Chinaco 114; Conquistador, El 116; Gran Centenario 121; Monte Alban 96, 146; Montezuma 124; Real Hacienda 130; Tres Magueyes 138; Two Fingers 141; Viuda de Romero 141,151